Janet and Richard Strombeck

MAKING TIMELESS TOYS IN WOOD

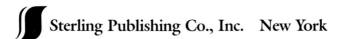

Sterling Publishing Co., Inc.   New York

Dedication

We dedicate this book to our valued customers who have shared their ideas and wants with us, and who make our day with their pictures, letters and comments.

Acknowledgments

We wish to thank again those people shown in the credits, for their talent and co-operation in assembling this book. We would also like to thank Christine Both and Kathy Redelings for their sewing and painting talents, and our grandchildren Adam and Kerry for all their "hands-on" testing.

Credits

Toy designs:
The Ströms

Book design:
Tessing Design

Photography:
Don Sala Photography

Illustration:
Marlene Ekman

Plans by:
Norma Schlosser

Published by:

Sterling Publishing Company, Inc.
387 Park Avenue South
New York, N.Y. 10016
Distributed in Canada by
Sterling Publishing
% Canadian Manda Group
P.O. Box 920, Station U
Toronto, Ontario, Canada M8Z 5P9
ISBN #0-912355-05-0

Printed in the U.S.A.

Foreword

As many of you already know, Sun Designs is a very small company which is dedicated to publishing designs and plans of unusual and hard-to-find things made from wood.

In keeping with that goal, we have developed what we think is an unusual collection of wood toys that the do-it-yourself woodworker can make for his children, grandchildren, or a good friend. Wood toys, of course, are so much more personal than synthetic ones and are easy to repair.

Many of the make-it-yourself toy books on the market today supply instructions for fairly quick toy projects. A significant number of our toys are also of relatively simple construction, but they are also very different and take more time; not because they are complicated, but because they have more detail and finishing to them.

A good number of the toys in this book can be completed with hand tools. For speed and convenience, we used both hand and power tools. Most of them were made from fir, and some of them from many fir scraps that have been glued together. Hardwood should be used for some toys such as Victoria and the buckets on the Hard Rock Mining Co.

We felt it impossible to have a full selection of designs with plans because of space limitations; so we have attempted to provide as much variety of subjects and designs as space permits, still allowing room for mini-plans of a good number of designs that lend themselves to a smaller space. We hope you like our selection.

If you have any questions, or need more information on these toys, please write or call us here at Sun Designs. Our telephone number is 414-567-4255.

We sincerely hope you enjoy our toys and make them as your toys. We also hope your children or grandchildren will have as much enjoyment from your efforts as ours have had.

IMPORTANT!
Please Read

We know that weather and supervision requirements of young children can limit their time outside; consequently, we have intended most of our toys to be used indoors. The obvious exceptions to this are the sleds, wagons, and the Hard Rock Mining Co. which is best used outside with silica sand. These outside items should be put together with waterproof glues, brass fasteners and finished with a spar varnish. It is also a good idea to put a rubber tread on the wheels of toys used outside.

Complete construction plans are available for all designs shown here, including ones shown as mini-plans. If a toy has a part(s) that we feel is not readily available at a local source, we made them available as an optional hardware package that may be bought separately. Most of the hardware we buy is from a local hardware store or one of a number of "catalog" companies.

Type of wood, design, and hardware are not rigid specifications. If you want to substitute plywood or have a better idea, (and we get pictures weekly as proof), please feel free to do so; and if you're not sure, just call us.

For your information, we have shown plan and optional hardware prices on page 96.

May you have good luck with all of your projects.

THE
STRÖM TOYS
AND PLANS

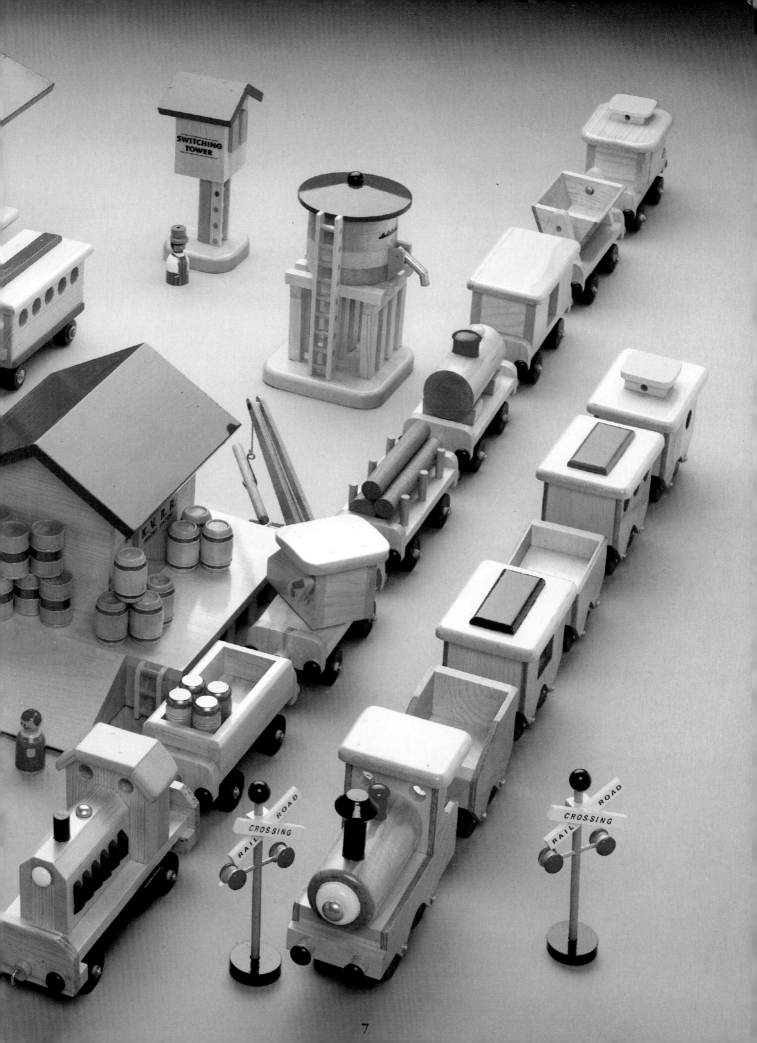

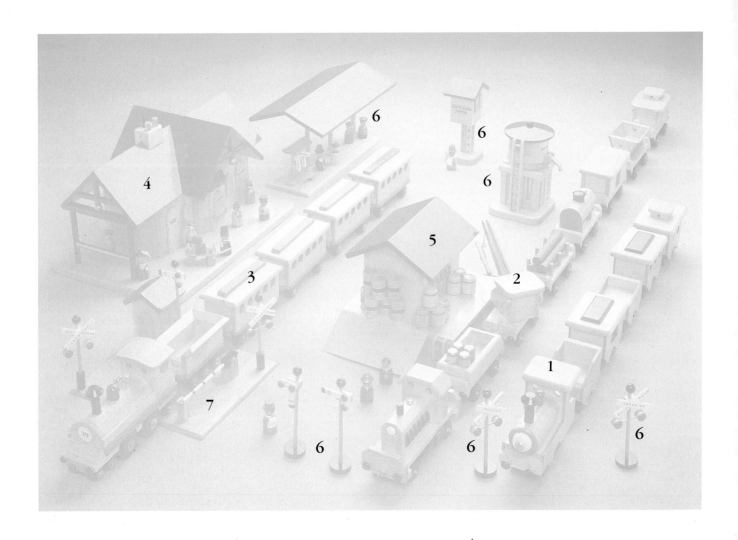

The Depot

As Stationmaster, some of your duties will include seeing that freight and baggage are properly loaded; directing passengers to the proper trains; selling tickets; and making sure the trains run on schedule and are properly maintained. Equipment can be duplicated for even more action and many years of continuous enjoyment. Truly a child's delight when they can say ALL ABOARD!

1 **Rocky Mountain Express** Old time train.

2 **Mohawk Valley Railway** Work train with engine and 7 cars.

3 **Federal Flyer** passenger train.

4 **Victorian Station**

5 **Freight Terminal**

6 **Depot Buildings & Access.** Switching & Water Towers, Waiting Platform, Crossing Accessories.

7 **Level Crossing**

Rocky Mountain Express

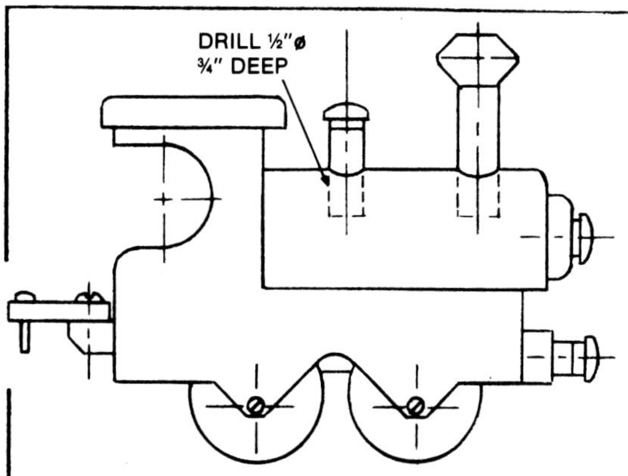

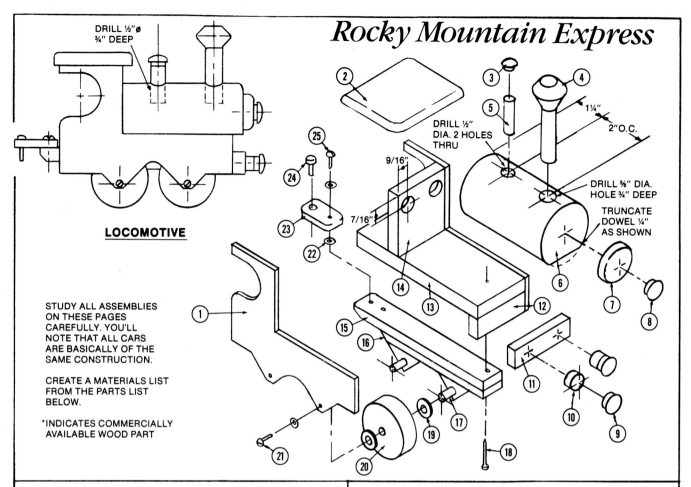

DRILL ½"ø
¾" DEEP

LOCOMOTIVE

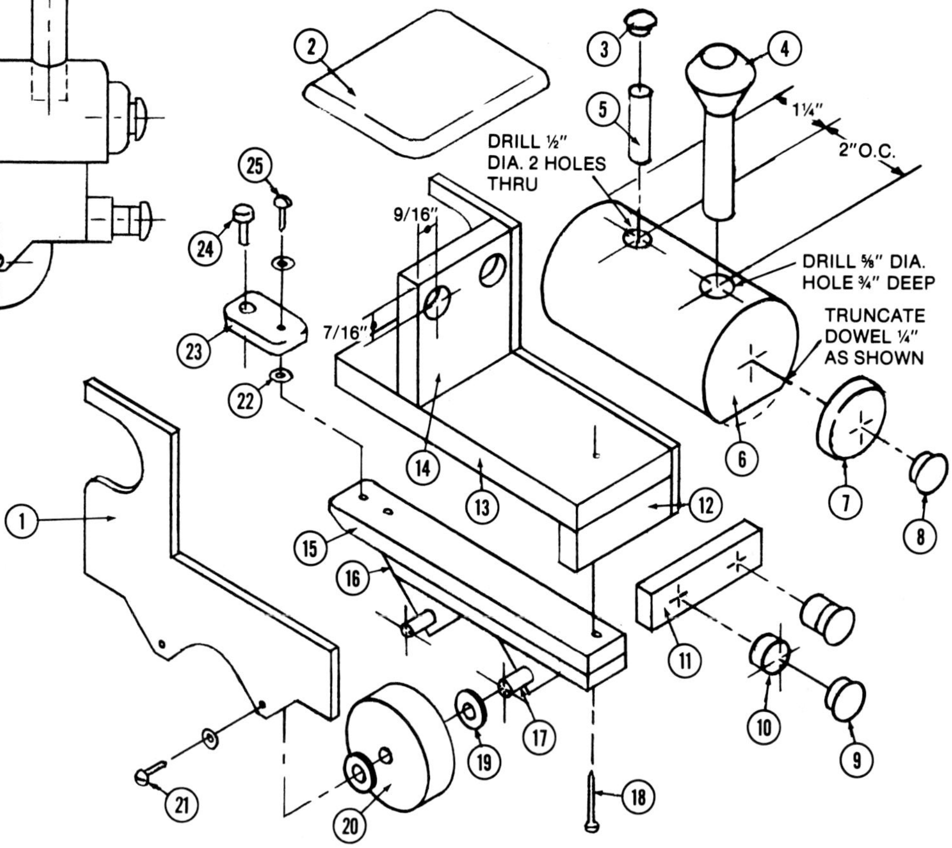

DRILL ½"
DIA. 2 HOLES
THRU
1¼"
2"O.C.
DRILL ⅝" DIA.
HOLE ¾" DEEP
TRUNCATE
DOWEL ¼"
AS SHOWN
9/16"
7/16"
1
2
3
4
5
6
7
8
9
10
11
12
13
14
15
16
17
18
19
20
21
22
23
24
25

STUDY ALL ASSEMBLIES ON THESE PAGES CAREFULLY. YOU'LL NOTE THAT ALL CARS ARE BASICALLY OF THE SAME CONSTRUCTION.

CREATE A MATERIALS LIST FROM THE PARTS LIST BELOW.

*INDICATES COMMERCIALLY AVAILABLE WOOD PART

PART	DESCRIPTION	MATL.	PCS.
1	SIDE WALL - SEE PG. 3	PLY.	2
2	ROOF - 2-13/16" x 3⅜"	½" (NOM.) PINE	
3	FURN. PLUG ½"	BIRCH	1
4	*STACK ⅝"ø x 2¾"	BIRCH	1
5	STACK ½"ø x 1⅜"	BIRCH	1
6	BOILER 2"ø x 4-5/16"	PINE	1
7	1¼" x ¼" DISC	PINE	1
8-9	FURN. PLUG ½"	BIRCH	3
10	½"ø x 5/16" DOWEL	BIRCH	2
11	7/16" x ¾" x 2⅞"	PINE	1
12	7/16" x ⅞" x 2⅜"	PINE	1
13	7/16" x 2⅜" x 6-3/16"	PINE	1
14	7/16" x 2⅜" x 2-7/16" H.	PINE	1
15	7/16" x 1⅛" x 6¼"	PINE	1
16	¼" x 1⅛" x 4⅝"	PINE	1
17	AXLE ¼"ø x 1"	BIRCH	24
18	¾" NO. 6 RD. HD. WD. SCR.	BRASS	12
19	FLAT WASHER ¼" I.D.	BRASS	42
20	ENG. WHEEL 2"ø x 7/16"	PINE	4
21	1" NO. 4 RD. HD. WD. SCR.	BRASS	24
22	FLAT WASHER ⅛" I.D.	BRASS	10
23	COUPLING - SEE PG. 3	PLY.	5
24	*AXLE PIN	BIRCH	5
25	¾" NO. 8 RD. HD. WD. SCR.	BRASS	5
26	SIDE WALL - SEE PG. 3	PLY.	10
27	END WALL 7/16" x 2⅜" x 2" H.	PINE	7
28	FLOOR 7/16" x 2⅜" x 3⅜" L.	PINE	5
29	END WALL 7/16" x 2⅜" x 1¼" H.	PINE	1
30	TONGUE 7/16" x 1⅛" W. x 1" L.	PINE	1
31	END WALL 7/16" x 2⅜" x 1¼" H.	PINE	2

- ALL CARS USE 1½" DIA. WHEELS CUT FROM ½" (NOM.) STOCK. 4 REQD. EA. CAR.

32	UNDERCARRIAGE, SEE PG. 3	PINE	5
33	ROOF 7/16" x 3½" W. x 5" L.	PINE	3
34	VENT ¼" x 1½" x 3½"	PLY.	2
35	BAY ¼" x 1½" x 2" H.	PLY.	2
36	VENT 7/16" x 1½" SQ.	PINE	1
37	COVER ¼" x 2" SQ.	PLY.	1

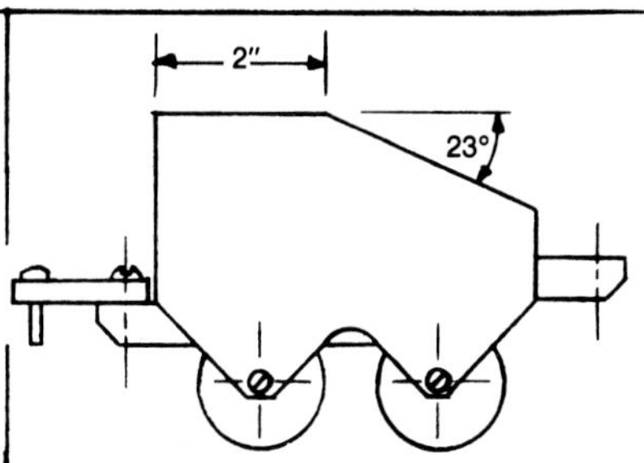

2"
23°

COAL TENDER

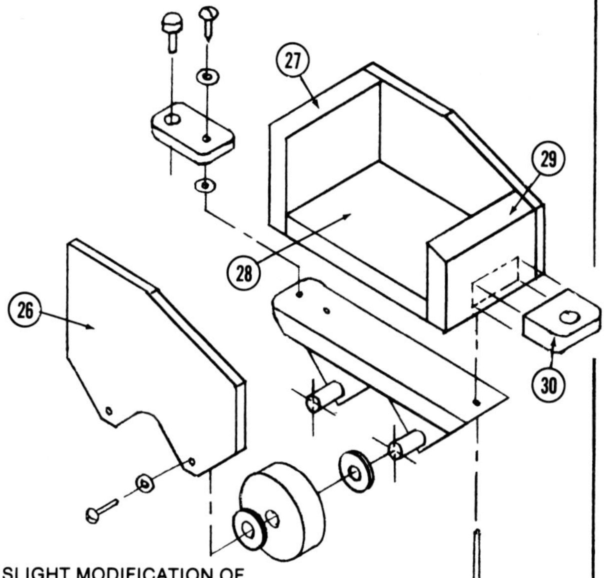

26
27
28
29
30

NOTE SLIGHT MODIFICATION OF UNDERCARRIAGE AND OFFSET COUPLING TONGUE, PART 30.

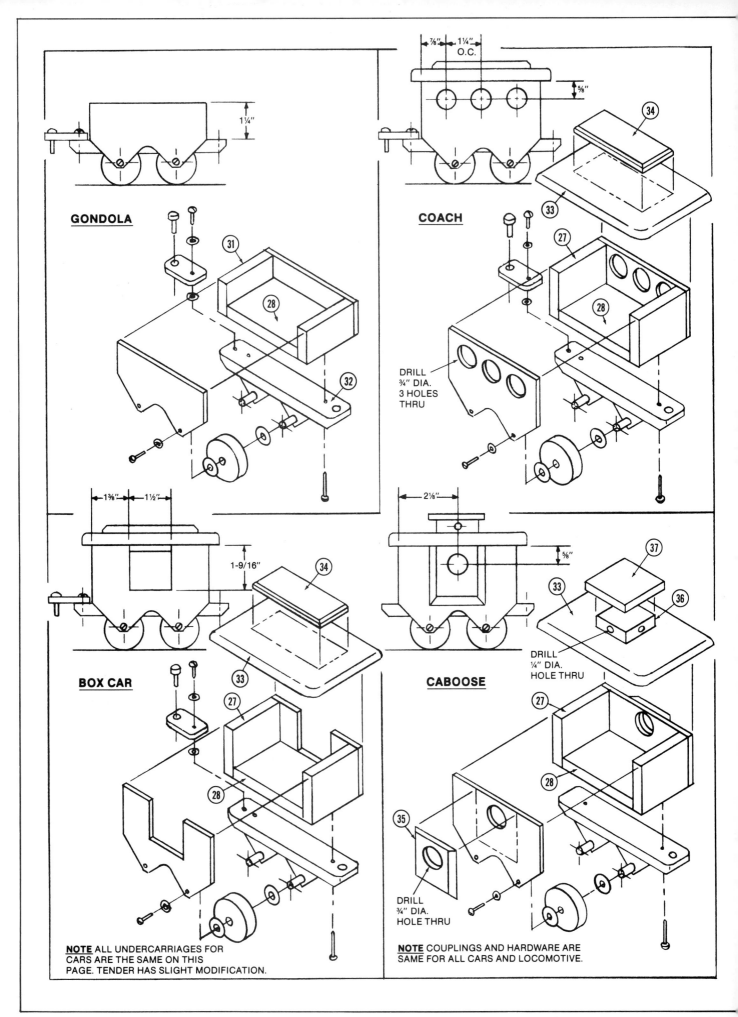

GONDOLA

COACH

DRILL
¾" DIA.
3 HOLES
THRU

BOX CAR

CABOOSE

DRILL
¼" DIA.
HOLE THRU

DRILL
¾" DIA.
HOLE THRU

NOTE ALL UNDERCARRIAGES FOR
CARS ARE THE SAME ON THIS
PAGE. TENDER HAS SLIGHT MODIFICATION.

NOTE COUPLINGS AND HARDWARE ARE
SAME FOR ALL CARS AND LOCOMOTIVE.

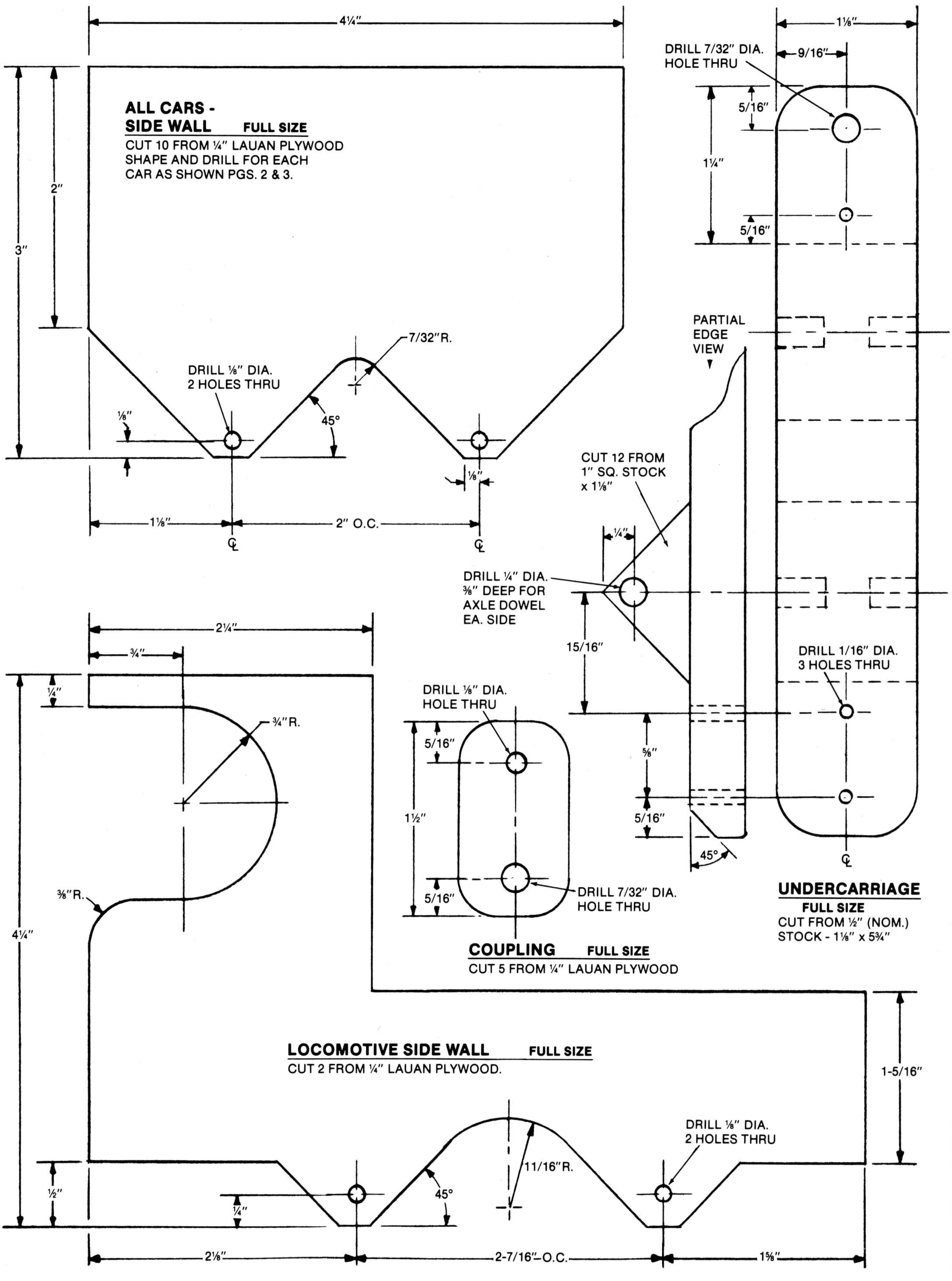

ALL CARS -
SIDE WALL FULL SIZE
CUT 10 FROM ¼" LAUAN PLYWOOD
SHAPE AND DRILL FOR EACH
CAR AS SHOWN PGS. 2 & 3.
4¼"
3"
2"
7/32"R.
DRILL ⅛" DIA.
2 HOLES THRU
45°
⅛"
⅛"
1⅛"
2" O.C.
℄
℄
1⅛"
DRILL 7/32" DIA.
HOLE THRU
9/16"
5/16"
1¼"
5/16"
PARTIAL
EDGE
VIEW
CUT 12 FROM
1" SQ. STOCK
x 1⅛"
¼"
DRILL ¼" DIA.
⅜" DEEP FOR
AXLE DOWEL
EA. SIDE
15/16"
DRILL 1/16" DIA.
3 HOLES THRU
⅝"
5/16"
45°
℄
UNDERCARRIAGE
FULL SIZE
CUT FROM ½" (NOM.)
STOCK - 1⅛" x 5¾"
DRILL ⅛" DIA.
HOLE THRU
5/16"
1½"
5/16"
DRILL 7/32" DIA.
HOLE THRU
COUPLING FULL SIZE
CUT 5 FROM ¼" LAUAN PLYWOOD
2¼"
¾"
¼"
¾"R.
⅜"R.
4¼"
LOCOMOTIVE SIDE WALL FULL SIZE
CUT 2 FROM ¼" LAUAN PLYWOOD.
1-5/16"
DRILL ⅛" DIA.
2 HOLES THRU
11/16"R.
45°
½"
¼"
2⅛"
2-7/16"-O.C.
1⅝"

Depot Buildings

NOTE:
STAIN & VARNISH AS DESIRED.
PAINT ROOF DARK BROWN.

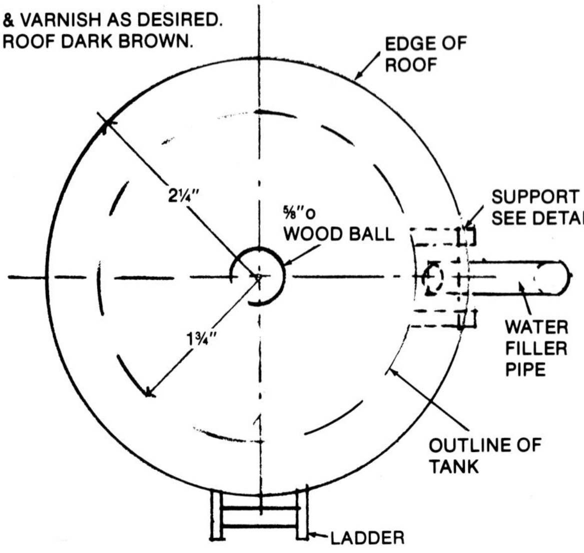

EDGE OF ROOF
2¼″
⅝″ø WOOD BALL
SUPPORT SEE DETAIL
WATER FILLER PIPE
1¾″
OUTLINE OF TANK
LADDER

TOP

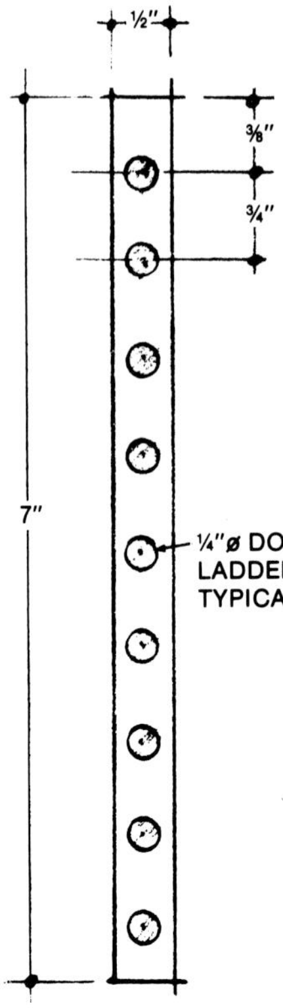

½″
⅜″
¾″
7″
¼″ø DOWEL LADDER RUNGS TYPICAL

LADDER

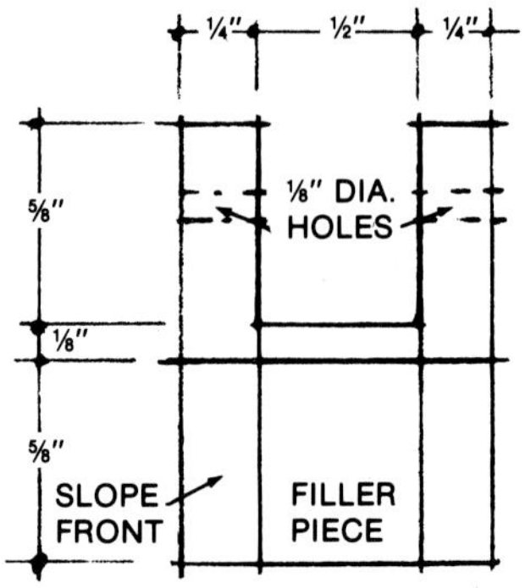

¼″
½″
¼″
⅝″
⅛″ DIA. HOLES
⅛″
⅝″
SLOPE FRONT
FILLER PIECE

SUPPORT - FRONT

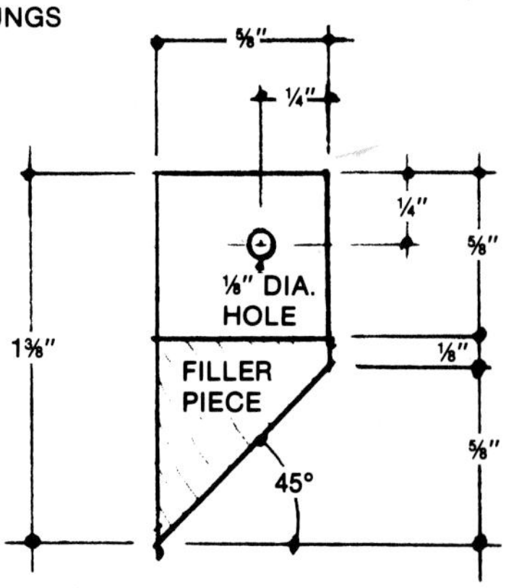

⅝″
¼″
¼″
⅝″
⅛″ DIA. HOLE
1⅜″
⅛″
FILLER PIECE
⅝″
45°

SUPPORT SECTION

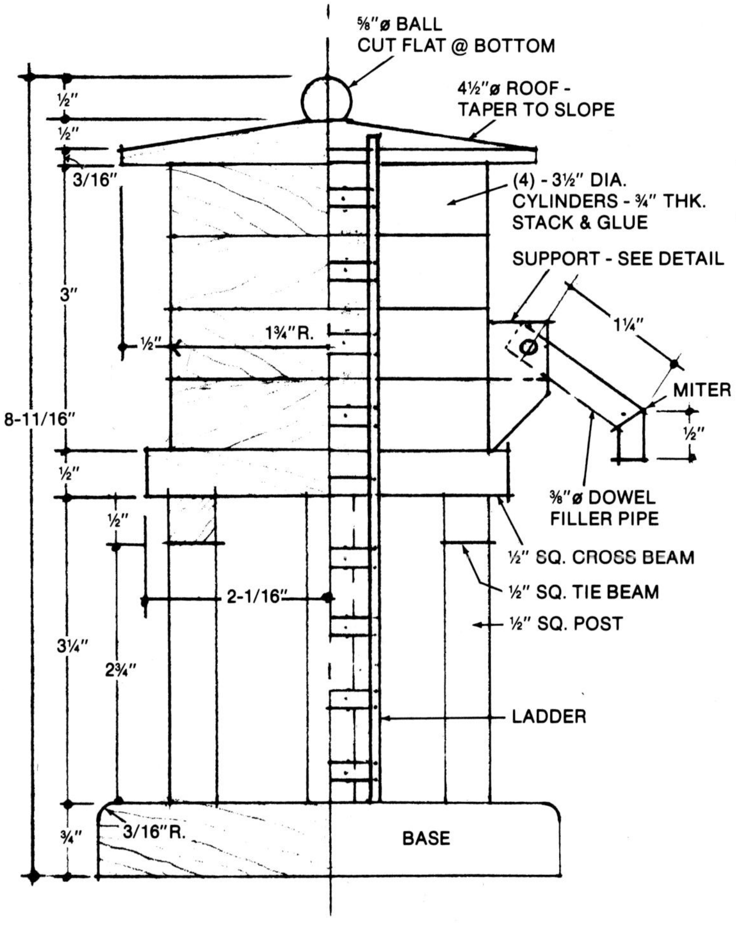

⅝″ø BALL CUT FLAT @ BOTTOM
4½″ø ROOF - TAPER TO SLOPE
½″
½″
3/16″
(4) - 3½″ DIA. CYLINDERS - ¾″ THK. STACK & GLUE
SUPPORT - SEE DETAIL
3″
1¼″
½″
1¾″R.
MITER
½″
8-11/16″
½″
⅜″ø DOWEL FILLER PIPE
½″
½″ SQ. CROSS BEAM
2-1/16″
½″ SQ. TIE BEAM
½″ SQ. POST
3¼″
2¾″
LADDER
¾″
3/16″R.
BASE

SECTION ELEVATION

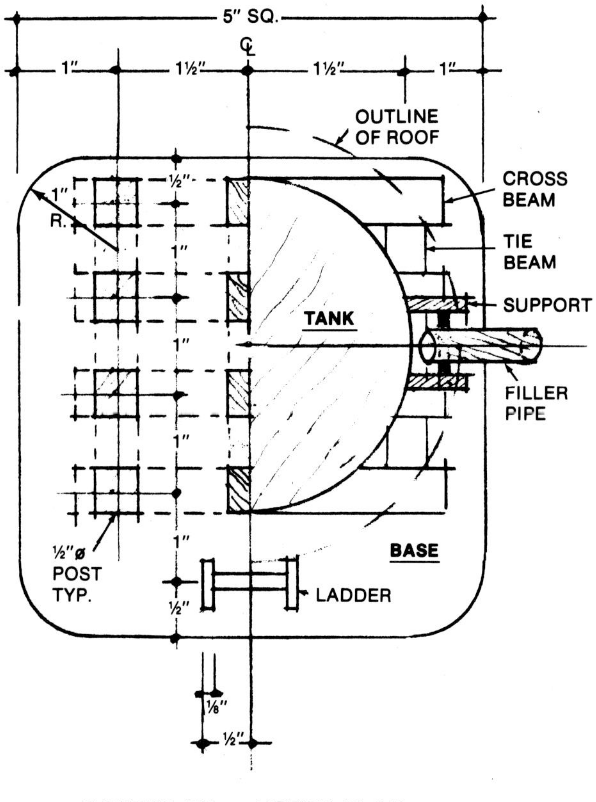

5″ SQ.
℄
1″
1½″
1½″
1″
OUTLINE OF ROOF
1″ R.
½″
CROSS BEAM
TIE BEAM
1″
SUPPORT
TANK
1″
FILLER PIPE
1″
1″
½″ø POST TYP.
BASE
LADDER
½″
⅛″
½″

BASE PLAN UPPER PLAN

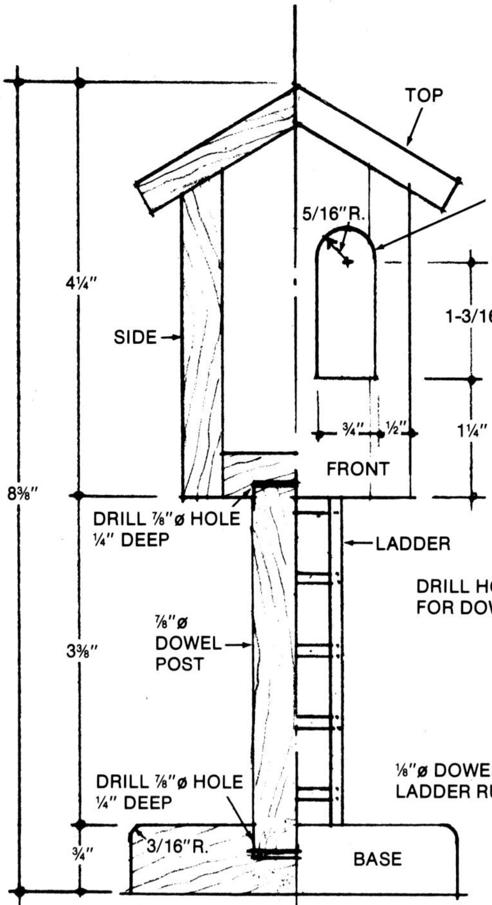
TOP
(2) ⅛" THICK WINDOW PANELS FRONT ONLY
5/16"R.
4¼"
SIDE
1-3/16"
¾"
½"
1¼"
FRONT
8⅜"
DRILL ⅞"ø HOLE ¼" DEEP
LADDER
⅞"ø DOWEL POST
3⅜"
DRILL ⅞"ø HOLE ¼" DEEP
3/16"R.
¾"
BASE

SECTION **ELEVATION**

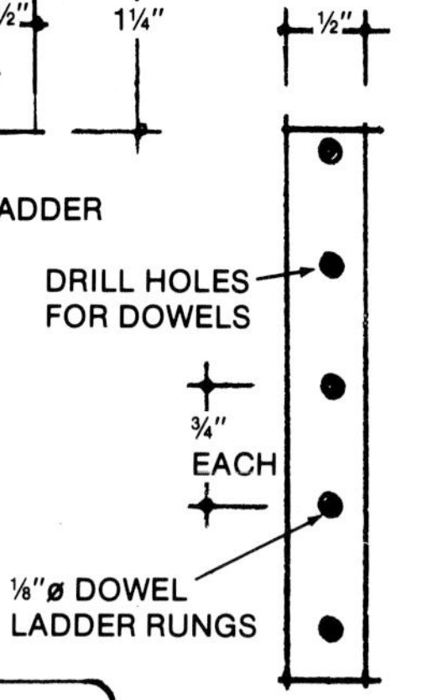
½"
DRILL HOLES FOR DOWELS
¾" EACH
⅛"ø DOWEL LADDER RUNGS

LADDER

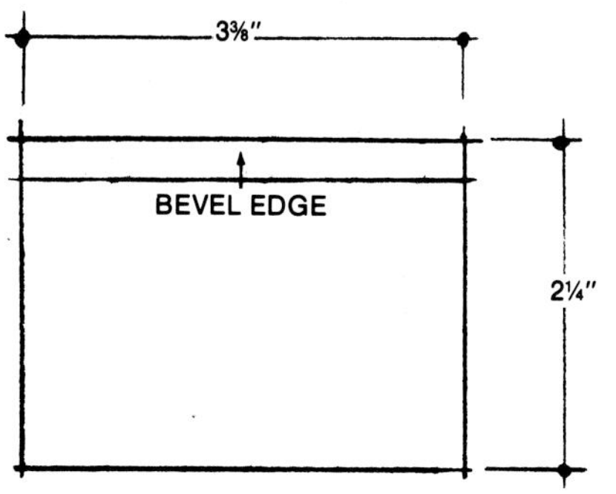
3⅜"
BEVEL EDGE
2¼"

TOP
2 EACH

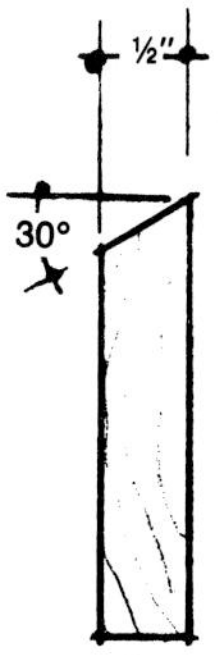
½"
30°

END

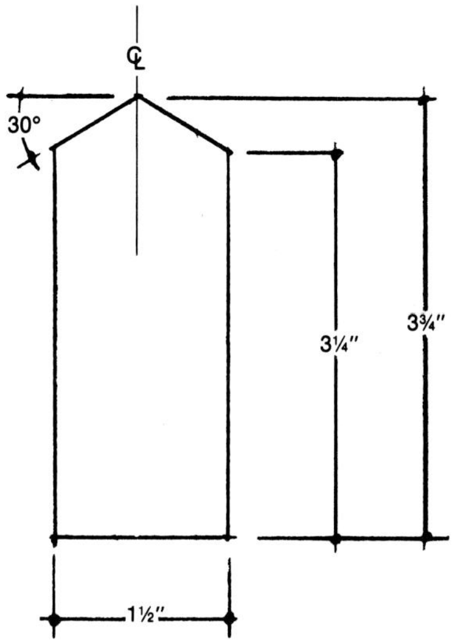
℄
30°
3¼"
3¾"
1½"

FRONT/BACK
1 EACH

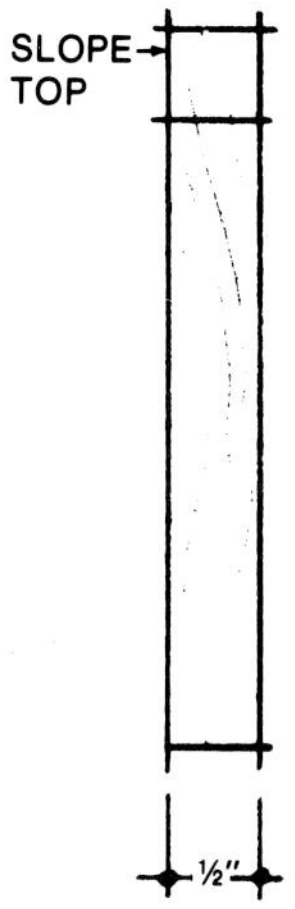
SLOPE TOP
½"

END

NOTE:
STAIN AND VARNISH AS DESIRED.
PAINT ROOF DARK BROWN.

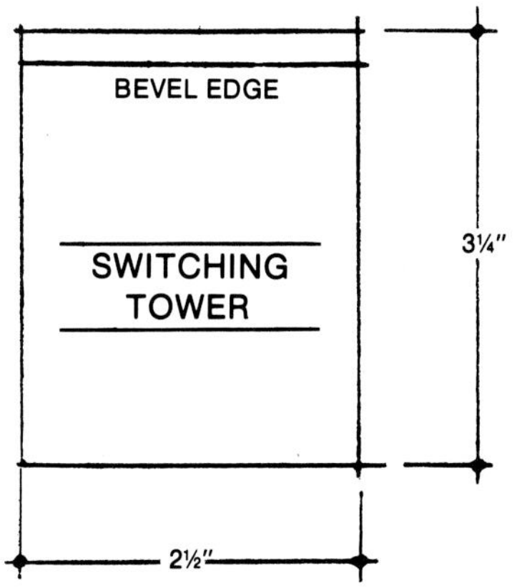
BEVEL EDGE
SWITCHING TOWER
3¼"
2½"

SIDE
2 EACH

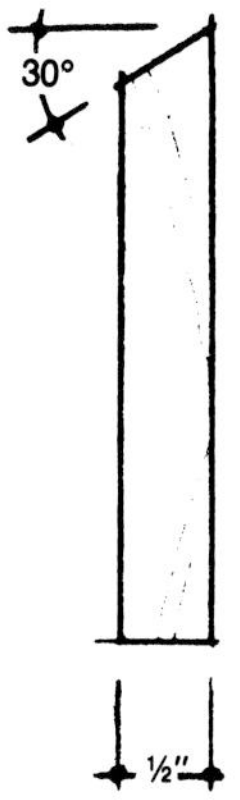
30°
½"

END

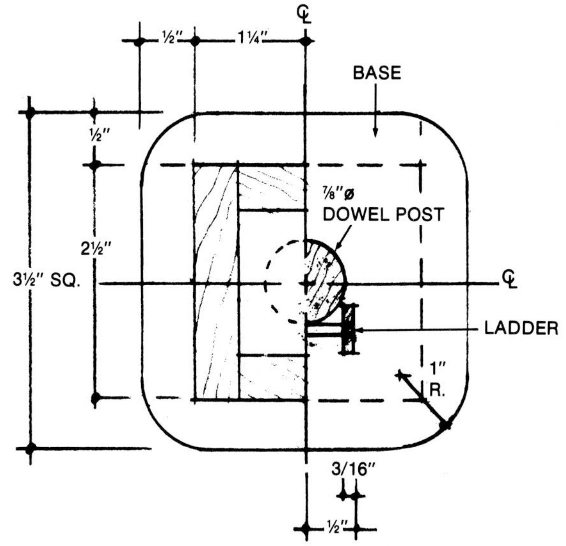
℄
½"
1¼"
BASE
½"
⅞"ø DOWEL POST
2½"
3½" SQ.
℄
LADDER
1" R.
3/16"
½"

UPPER PLAN **BASE PLAN**

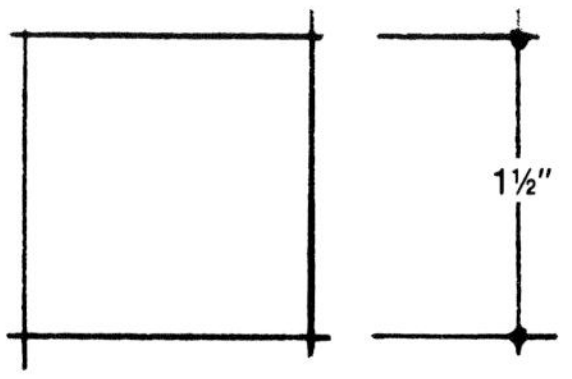
1½"

BOTTOM

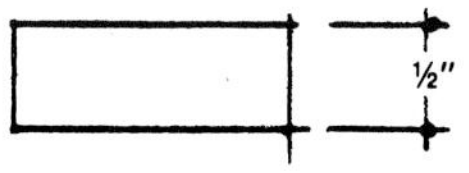
½"

END

Leigh's Comfort Rocker

Apopular favorite with everyone, and the perfect place to be when visiting, feeding baby, reading, or resting. Just different enough in design to add a distinctive note to your other furnishings.

Size: 14½" wide
21" deep
25" high

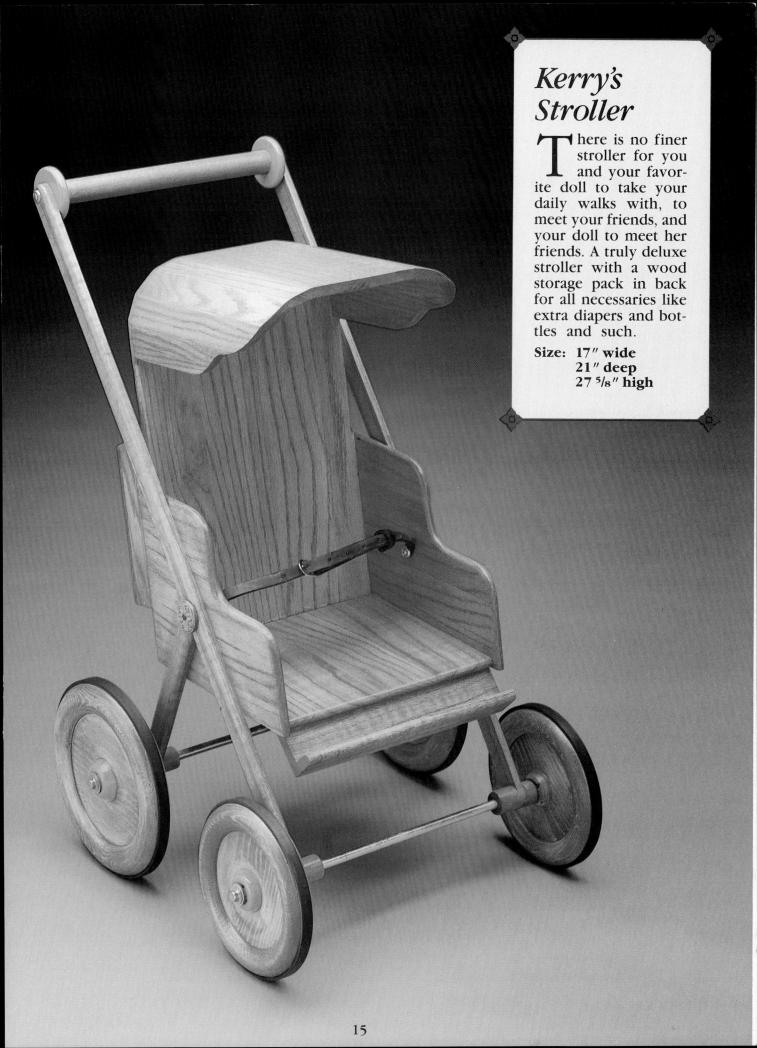

Kerry's Stroller

There is no finer stroller for you and your favorite doll to take your daily walks with, to meet your friends, and your doll to meet her friends. A truly deluxe stroller with a wood storage pack in back for all necessaries like extra diapers and bottles and such.

Size: 17" wide
21" deep
27 5/8" high

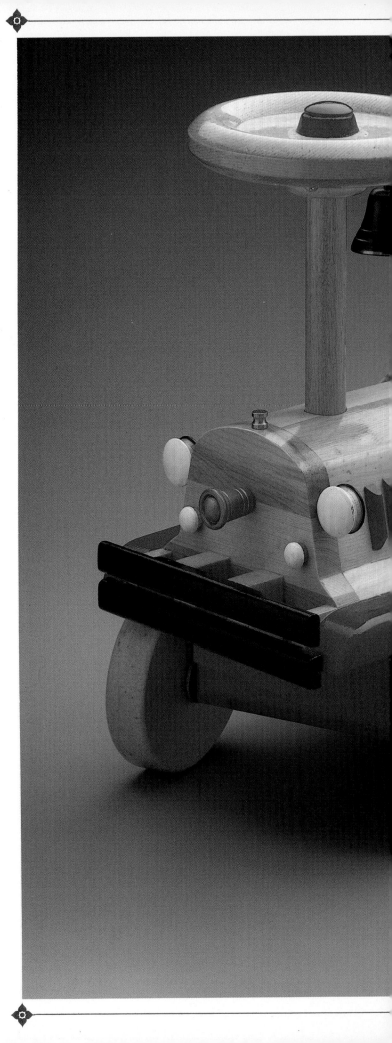

Fire Engine

These firemen are ready for action and waiting for a driver. Is he someone you know? He'll find this truck fully equipped with over 5′ of hose that attaches to brass connections on side of truck, two ladders, full equipment storage under driver's seat, and even 2 fender-mounted fire extinguishers. Sure could be a lot of fun for someone you know!

Size: **31″ long**
11 1/2″ wide
9 1/2″ high, seat
17 1/2″ high, to top of wheel

Saturday Morning Moving Van

A neat little truck for 2-year olds and up to ride. Back doors open to store treasures. Turns easily and will "move" you quickly wherever you want to go.

Size: **15³/₄" high**
11¹/₂" wide
26" long

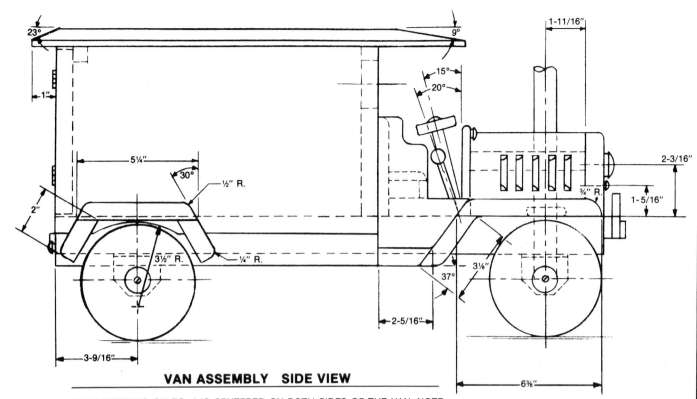

VAN ASSEMBLY   SIDE VIEW

THE LETTERING ON PG. 4 IS CENTERED ON BOTH SIDES OF THE VAN. NOTE THAT THE UNDERCARRIAGE FORMS THE FLOOR OF THE VAN.

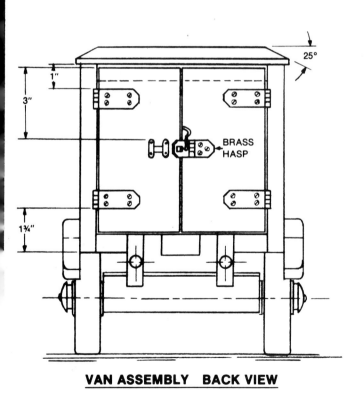

VAN ASSEMBLY   BACK VIEW

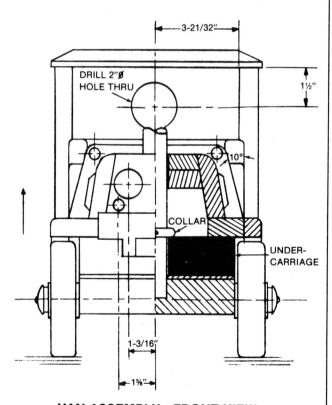

VAN ASSEMBLY   FRONT VIEW

NOTE THAT THE ENGINE BLOCK & CAB ASSEMBLY IS NOT NAILED OR GLUED TO THE UNDERCARRIAGE OF VAN. THIS IS TO ALLOW YOU TO LIFT UP THE ASSEMBLY TO GIVE ACCESS TO THE STEERING COLUMN COLLAR. PUT SCREW IN CAB FLOOR BOARD TO HOLD SECURELY, BUT STILL HAVE ASSEMBLY REMOVABLE.

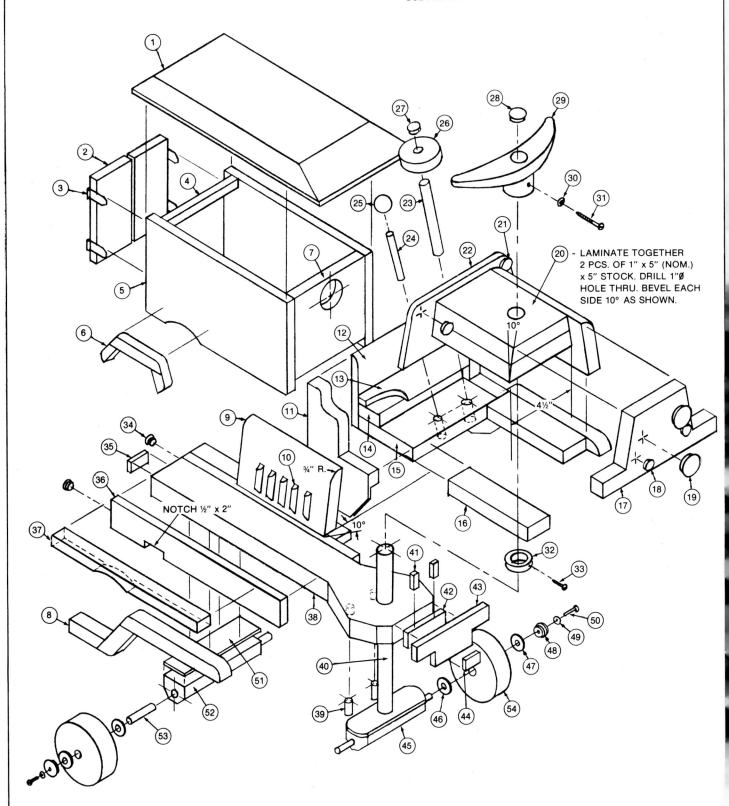

20 - LAMINATE TOGETHER
2 PCS. OF 1" x 5" (NOM.)
x 5" STOCK. DRILL 1"Ø
HOLE THRU. BEVEL EACH
SIDE 10° AS SHOWN.

10°

4½"

¾" R.

NOTCH ½" x 2"

10°

VAN ASSEMBLY

PART	DESCRIPTION	MATL.	PCS.
1	VAN TOP - ¾" x 9" x 18⅝"	PINE	1
2	DOOR - ¾" x 3½" x 6⅞"	PINE	2
3	STRAP HINGE - 1¾"	BRASS	2 Pr.
4	DOOR STOP ¾" SQ. x 7-5/16"	PINE	1
5	VAN SIDE - ¾" x 7¾" x 13-15/16"	PINE	2
6	FENDER ASSEMBLY, PG. 3	PINE	2
7	VAN FRONT - ¾" x 7-5/16" x 7" h.	PINE	1
8	FENDER ASSEMBLY, PG. 3	PINE	2
9	ENG. BLK. SIDE - ¾" x 2⅞" x 5¾"	PINE	2
10	GRILL WORK - ¼" QUARTER RD. x 1½"	PINE	10
11	CAB SIDE - ¾" x 3⅞" x 6"	PINE	2
12	SEAT BACK - ⅜" x 4" x 6"	PINE	1
13	SEAT - ⅜" x 1⅝" x 6"	PINE	1
14	SEAT BLK. - ¾" x 1⅜" x 6"	PINE	1
15	CAB FLOOR - ¾" x 3½" x 6"	PINE	1
16	ENG. BLK. BASE - ¾" x 1½" x 5"	PINE	2
17	ENG. BLK. FRONT - ¾" x 3½" x 7½"	PINE	1
18	LIGHTS - ⅜" FURNITURE PLUG	BIRCH	2
19	HEADLIGHTS - 1" FURNITURE PLUG	BIRCH	2
20	ENGINE BLOCK TOP - SEE NOTE	PINE	1
21	LIGHTS - ⅜" FURNITURE PLUG	BIRCH	2
22	DASHBOARD - ⅜" x 3-1/16" x 7½"	PINE	1
23	DOWEL - ½"Ø x 4"	BIRCH	1
24	DOWEL - 5/16"Ø x 2⅝"	BIRCH	1
25	WOOD BALL - ⅝"Ø	BIRCH	1
26	WHEEL, DOWEL - 1¾"Ø x ½"	BIRCH	1
27	HORN - ½" FURNITURE PLUG	BIRCH	1
28	HORN - 1" FURNITURE PLUG	BIRCH	1
29	HANDLE - SEE PAGE 4	PINE	1
30	FLAT WASHER - ⅛" I.D.	BRASS	1
31	2" NO. 8 RD. HD. WOOD SCREW	BRASS	1
32	COLLAR - 1" I.D. MACRAME RING	PINE	1
33	¾" NO. 6 RD. HD. WOOD SCREW	BRASS	1
34	TAIL LIGHT - ½" FURNITURE PLUG	BIRCH	2
35	LICENSE PLATE - 5/16" x ⅞" x 1⅝"	PINE	1
36	FRAME - ¾" x 2⅛" x 17-1/16"	PINE	2
37	WHEEL WELL STRIP - ¾" x 1⅜" x 14⅞"	PINE	2
38	UNDERCARRIAGE, PAGE 4	PINE	1
39	AXLE STOP, DOWEL - ⅜"Ø x 1"	BIRCH	2
40	STEERING COLUMN, DOWEL 1"Ø x 13½"	BIRCH	1
41	BUMPER BLOCKS - ½" SQ. x 1⅛"	PINE	2
42	BUMPER SUPPORT - ½" x 1¼" x 3½"L.	PINE	1
43	BUMPER - ½" x 2⅜" x 6⅝"L.	PINE	1
44	LICENSE PLATE - 5/16" x ⅞" x 1⅝"	PINE	1
45	FRONT AXLE, PAGE 4	PINE	1
46 & 47	FLAT WASHER - 9/16" I.D.	BRASS	8
48	HUB - 1" FURNITURE PLUG	BIRCH	4
49	FLAT WASHER - ⅛" I.D.	BRASS	4
50	1" NO. 6 RD. HD. WOOD SCREW	BRASS	4
51	AXLE COVER - ⅛" x 2" x 7-11/16"	PINE	1
52	BACK AXLE - 1½" x 2" x 7-11/16"	PINE	1
53	AXLE, DOWEL - ½"Ø x 2"	BIRCH	4
54	WHEEL - 1⅛" x 4¾" DIA.	PINE	4

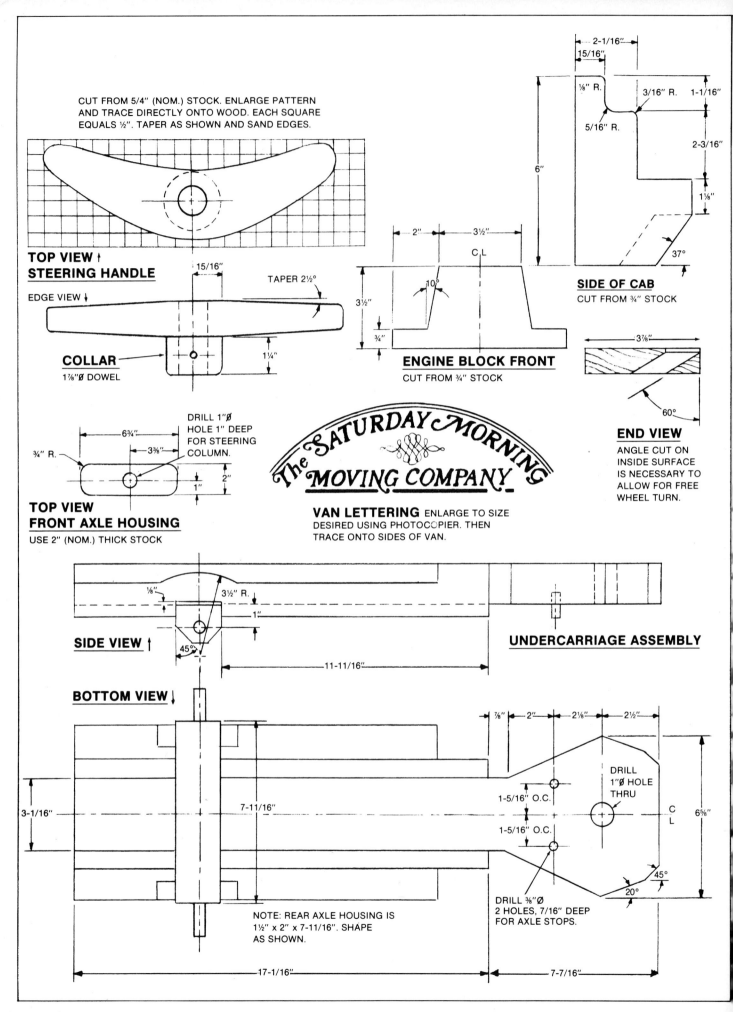

CUT FROM 5/4" (NOM.) STOCK. ENLARGE PATTERN AND TRACE DIRECTLY ONTO WOOD. EACH SQUARE EQUALS ½". TAPER AS SHOWN AND SAND EDGES.

TOP VIEW
STEERING HANDLE

EDGE VIEW ↓

15/16"

TAPER 2½°

COLLAR
1⅞"Ø DOWEL

1¼"

SIDE OF CAB
CUT FROM ¾" STOCK

2-1/16"
15/16"
⅛" R.
3/16" R.
1-1/16"
5/16" R.
6"
2-3/16"
1⅛"
37°

2"   3½"
C L

3½"

¾"

10°

ENGINE BLOCK FRONT
CUT FROM ¾" STOCK

3⅞"

60°

END VIEW
ANGLE CUT ON INSIDE SURFACE IS NECESSARY TO ALLOW FOR FREE WHEEL TURN.

DRILL 1"Ø HOLE 1" DEEP FOR STEERING COLUMN.

6¾"
¾" R.
3⅜"
2"
1"

TOP VIEW
FRONT AXLE HOUSING
USE 2" (NOM.) THICK STOCK

The SATURDAY MORNING
MOVING COMPANY

VAN LETTERING ENLARGE TO SIZE DESIRED USING PHOTOCOPIER. THEN TRACE ONTO SIDES OF VAN.

⅛"
3½" R.
1"

SIDE VIEW ↑

45°

11-11/16"

UNDERCARRIAGE ASSEMBLY

BOTTOM VIEW ↓

⅞"   2"   2⅛"   2½"

DRILL 1"Ø HOLE THRU

1-5/16" O.C.

7-11/16"

3-1/16"

1-5/16" O.C.

C L

6⅝"

45°

20°

DRILL ⅜"Ø 2 HOLES, 7/16" DEEP FOR AXLE STOPS.

NOTE: REAR AXLE HOUSING IS 1½" x 2" x 7-11/16". SHAPE AS SHOWN.

17-1/16"

7-7/16"

Elizabeth

Wouldn't any doll feel like a princess lying in this gorgeous cradle? Its smooth, swinging motion will lull her to sleep quickly. Plans include patterns for pad and pillow.

**Size: 28¹⁄₂″ long
14″ wide
29″ high**

School Bus

A great toy young-sters readily associate and play with while wait-ing for the real thing. Top lifts up for taking students and bus driver out. Turns and rides easily.

Size: 24" long
9" wide
12" high
17" to top of steering wheel

Sarah's Stove

For every young homemaker. A cooking stove with knobs that turn, removable baking racks in both ovens, and a large storage drawer for pots, pans and treasures. Accessory food items from Pine Branch Bakery available.

Size: **36″ high**
29″ wide
16″ deep

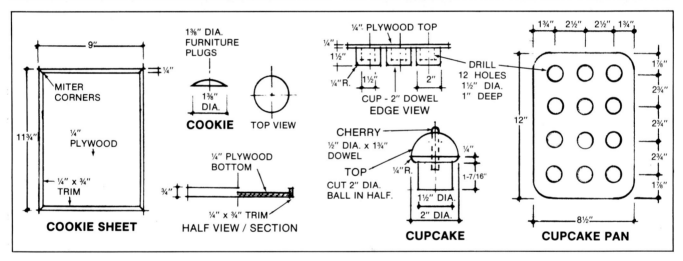

COOKIE SHEET

1⅜" DIA. FURNITURE PLUGS

1⅜" DIA.

COOKIE

TOP VIEW

9"

¼"

MITER CORNERS

¼" PLYWOOD

11¾"

¼" x ¾" TRIM

¼" PLYWOOD BOTTOM

¾"

¼" x ¾" TRIM

HALF VIEW / SECTION

¼" PLYWOOD TOP

¼"

1½"

¼" R.

1½"

2"

CUP - 2" DOWEL

EDGE VIEW

DRILL 12 HOLES 1½" DIA. 1" DEEP

CHERRY

½" DIA. x 1¾" DOWEL

TOP

¼" R.

¼"

1-7/16"

CUT 2" DIA. BALL IN HALF.

1½" DIA.

2" DIA.

CUPCAKE

1¾" 2½" 2½" 1¾"

1⅞"

2¾"

2¾"

2¾"

1⅞"

12"

8½"

CUPCAKE PAN

Cookies and Cookie Tin

What kind of cookies do you like? Well, then that's the kind we'll make. All we need is a cookie tin and some round cookie dough from Andrea's Pine Branch Bakery, some decorating materials, and we're all set. Perfect cookies come out of Sarah's Stove every time.

Size: Cookie Tin: 9″ wide
11¾″ long
¾″ high

Cookies: 1⅜″ diameter

Cupcake Tin and Cupcakes

At last, the secret recipe from the Pine Branch Bakery for making perfect cupcakes and muffins every time. They can be decorated in any flavor or even for special events like birthdays. Now really, is any party really a party without cupcakes? Of course, we'll give you the instructions for the cooking tin at the same time.

Size: Cupcake Tin: 1¹³⁄₁₆″ high
8½″ wide
12″ long

Cupcakes: 2½″ high
2″ wide

Food Puzzles

Birthday Cake Puzzle
Any good cook can finish this birthday cake recipe. Each slice has 3 separate pieces to fit together, besides the candle, so maybe you'll want to number them.

Pinecrust Bread A tasty, all natural, presliced loaf of bread that can only be from Andrea's Pinebranch Bakery. Perfect for peanut butter and jam.

Pie Puzzle Of course, no dinner is complete without dessert.

Rebbecca's Icebox

An old-time ice-box sized to match the stove. It has an upper compartment to hold plenty of ice and a lower compartment complete with food shelf and door rack. Of course, both compartments are a good place to store "stuff".

Size: 40$^{1}/_{2}$" high
21" wide
15" deep

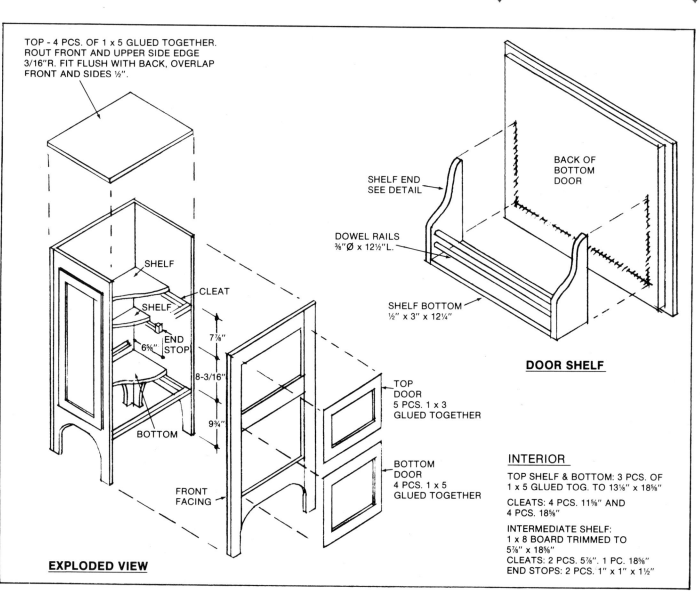

TOP - 4 PCS. OF 1 x 5 GLUED TOGETHER. ROUT FRONT AND UPPER SIDE EDGE 3/16"R. FIT FLUSH WITH BACK, OVERLAP FRONT AND SIDES ½".

BACK OF BOTTOM DOOR

SHELF END SEE DETAIL

DOWEL RAILS ⅜"Ø x 12½"L.

SHELF BOTTOM ½" x 3" x 12¼"

DOOR SHELF

SHELF

CLEAT

SHELF

END STOP

6⅝"

7⅞"

8-3/16"

9¾"

BOTTOM

FRONT FACING

TOP DOOR 5 PCS. 1 x 3 GLUED TOGETHER

BOTTOM DOOR 4 PCS. 1 x 5 GLUED TOGETHER

INTERIOR

TOP SHELF & BOTTOM: 3 PCS. OF 1 x 5 GLUED TOG. TO 13⅛" x 18⅝"

CLEATS: 4 PCS. 11⅝" AND 4 PCS. 18⅝"

INTERMEDIATE SHELF: 1 x 8 BOARD TRIMMED TO 5⅞" x 18⅝"
CLEATS: 2 PCS. 5⅞". 1 PC. 18⅝"
END STOPS: 2 PCS. 1" x 1" x 1½"

EXPLODED VIEW

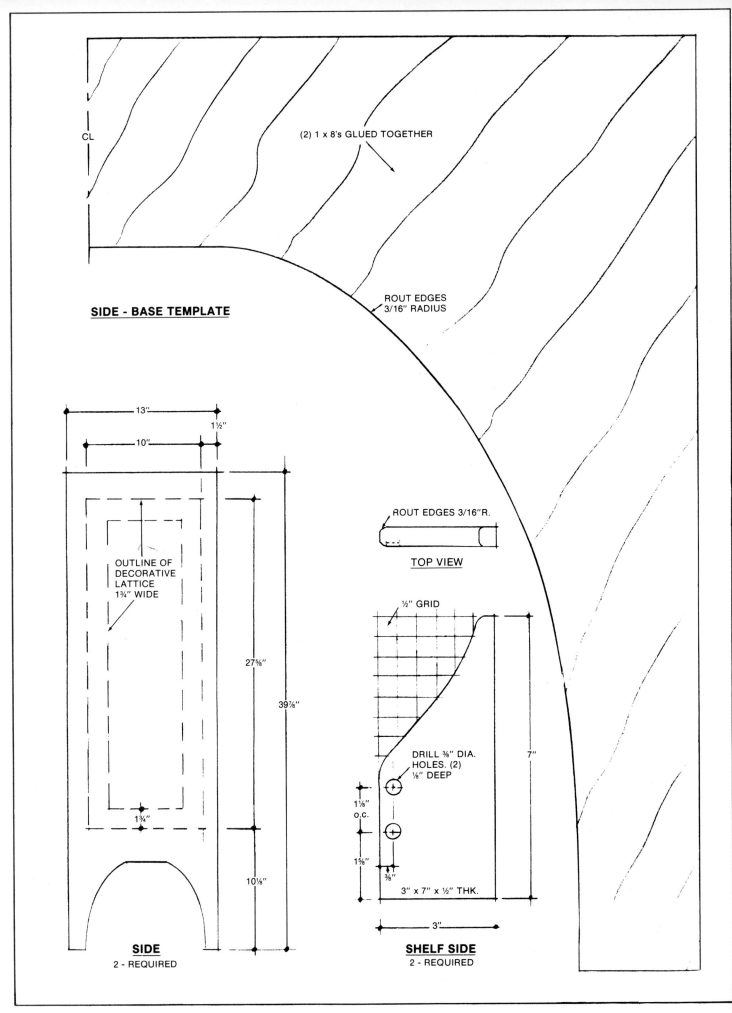

(2) 1 x 8's GLUED TOGETHER

CL

SIDE - BASE TEMPLATE

ROUT EDGES
3/16" RADIUS

13"

1½"

10"

OUTLINE OF
DECORATIVE
LATTICE
1¾" WIDE

27⅝"

39⅞"

ROUT EDGES 3/16"R.

TOP VIEW

½" GRID

1¾"

DRILL ⅜" DIA.
HOLES. (2)
⅛" DEEP

1⅛"
o.c.

1⅝"

⅜"

7"

3" x 7" x ½" THK.

10⅛"

3"

SIDE
2 - REQUIRED

SHELF SIDE
2 - REQUIRED

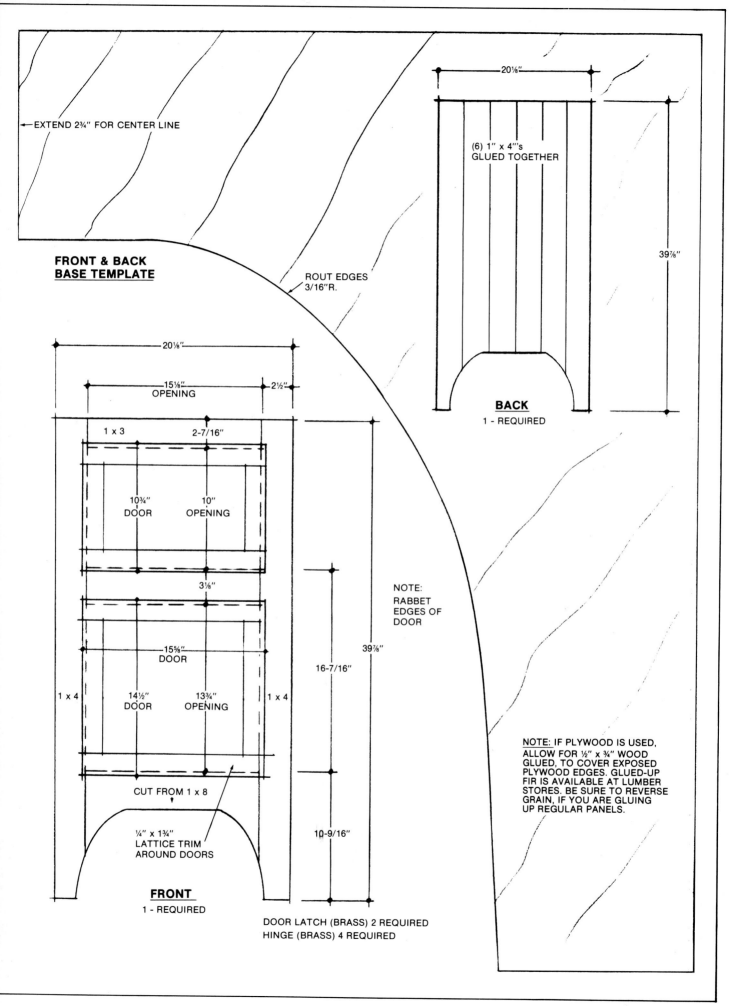

← EXTEND 2¾" FOR CENTER LINE

**FRONT & BACK
BASE TEMPLATE**

ROUT EDGES
3/16"R.

20⅛"

(6) 1" x 4"'s
GLUED TOGETHER

39⅞"

BACK
1 - REQUIRED

20⅛"

15⅛"
OPENING

2½"

1 x 3

2-7/16"

10¾"
DOOR

10"
OPENING

3⅛"

15⅝"
DOOR

14½"
DOOR

13¾"
OPENING

1 x 4

1 x 4

16-7/16"

39⅞"

10-9/16"

NOTE:
RABBET
EDGES OF
DOOR

CUT FROM 1 x 8

¼" x 1¾"
LATTICE TRIM
AROUND DOORS

FRONT
1 - REQUIRED

DOOR LATCH (BRASS) 2 REQUIRED
HINGE (BRASS) 4 REQUIRED

NOTE: IF PLYWOOD IS USED,
ALLOW FOR ½" x ¾" WOOD
GLUED, TO COVER EXPOSED
PLYWOOD EDGES. GLUED-UP
FIR IS AVAILABLE AT LUMBER
STORES. BE SURE TO REVERSE
GRAIN, IF YOU ARE GLUING
UP REGULAR PANELS.

31

Play Center

Combined toy chest, blackboard, desk, bookshelves, crayon holder and storage for all kinds of treasures. Almost everything they need in one convenient, beautiful piece of furniture. Any child would surely love this!

Size: **47″ high**
     29¹/₂″ wide
     17¹/₂″ depth

Play Center

PART	DESCRIPTION	MATL.	PCS.
1.	DECORATIVE TRIM	PINE	1
2.	TOP ¾" x 12¾" x 29½"	PINE	1
3.	SIDE TRIM ¾" x 1½" x 11½"	PINE	2
4.	BACK ½" x 27⅞" x 42"	INT. PLY	1
5.	SIDE ¾" x 11⅛" x 42"	PINE	2
6.	SIDE ⅜" x 6½" x 16⅞"	PINE	2
7.	LG. DIVIDER ⅜" x 6½" x 5⅝"H.	PINE	1
8.	SHELF ⅜" x 6½" x 12"	PINE	3
9.	SM. DIVIDER ⅜" x 6½" x 3¼"H.	PINE	2
10.	LG. SHELF ¾" x 10⅝" x 27"	PINE	1
11.	DRAWER SIDE ⅜" x 2⅞" x 6"	PINE	2
12.	DRAWER BOTTOM ⅜" x 6¾" x 11⅞"	PINE	1
13.	DRAWER SIDE ⅜" x 2⅞" x 11⅞"	PINE	2
14.	SM. LETTERS ½" HIGH	PLASTIC	

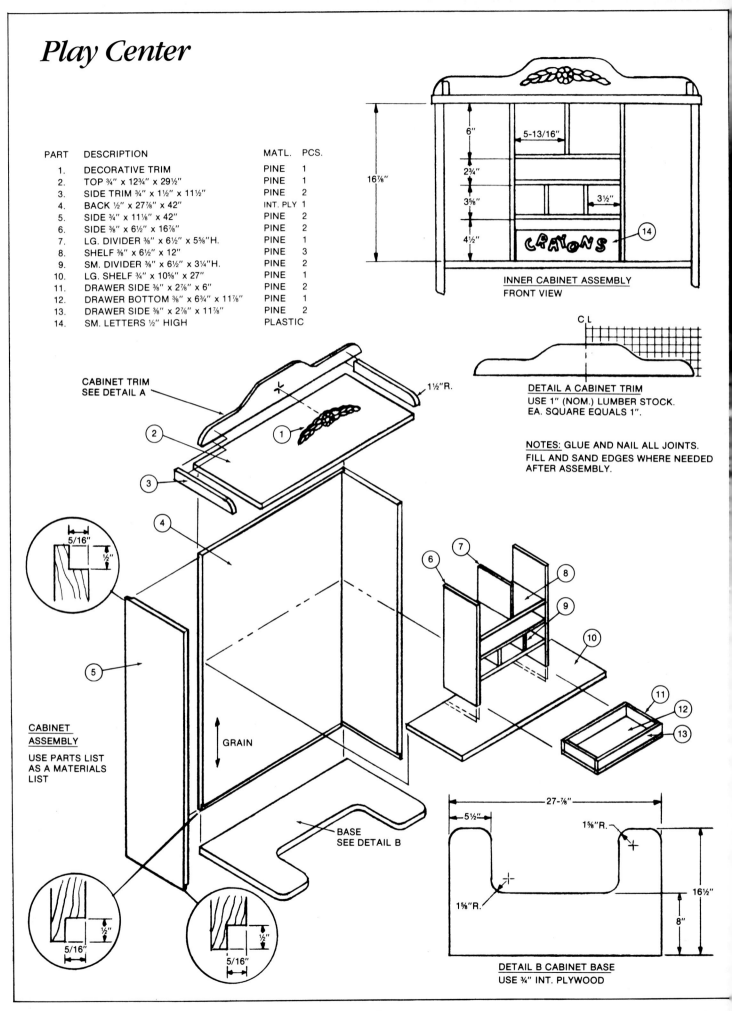

INNER CABINET ASSEMBLY
FRONT VIEW

CABINET TRIM
SEE DETAIL A

1½"R.

DETAIL A CABINET TRIM
USE 1" (NOM.) LUMBER STOCK.
EA. SQUARE EQUALS 1".

NOTES: GLUE AND NAIL ALL JOINTS.
FILL AND SAND EDGES WHERE NEEDED
AFTER ASSEMBLY.

CABINET
ASSEMBLY

USE PARTS LIST
AS A MATERIALS
LIST

GRAIN

BASE
SEE DETAIL B

DETAIL B CABINET BASE
USE ¾" INT. PLYWOOD

27-⅞"
5½"
1⅝"R.
1⅝"R.
16½"
8"

5/16"
½"

34

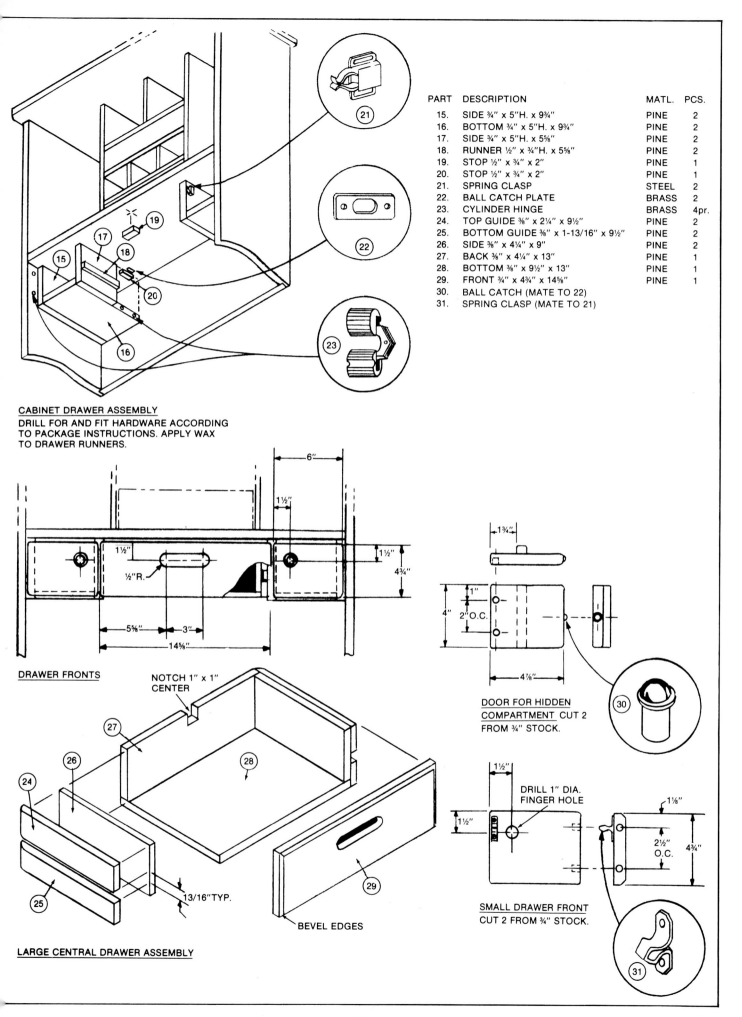

PART	DESCRIPTION	MATL.	PCS.
15.	SIDE ¾" x 5"H. x 9¾"	PINE	2
16.	BOTTOM ¾" x 5"H. x 9¾"	PINE	2
17.	SIDE ¾" x 5"H. x 5⅝"	PINE	2
18.	RUNNER ½" x ¾"H. x 5⅝"	PINE	2
19.	STOP ½" x ¾" x 2"	PINE	1
20.	STOP ½" x ¾" x 2"	PINE	1
21.	SPRING CLASP	STEEL	2
22.	BALL CATCH PLATE	BRASS	2
23.	CYLINDER HINGE	BRASS	4pr.
24.	TOP GUIDE ⅜" x 2¼" x 9½"	PINE	2
25.	BOTTOM GUIDE ⅜" x 1-13/16" x 9½"	PINE	2
26.	SIDE ⅜" x 4¼" x 9"	PINE	2
27.	BACK ⅜" x 4¼" x 13"	PINE	1
28.	BOTTOM ⅜" x 9½" x 13"	PINE	1
29.	FRONT ¾" x 4¾" x 14⅝"	PINE	1
30.	BALL CATCH (MATE TO 22)		
31.	SPRING CLASP (MATE TO 21)		

CABINET DRAWER ASSEMBLY
DRILL FOR AND FIT HARDWARE ACCORDING TO PACKAGE INSTRUCTIONS. APPLY WAX TO DRAWER RUNNERS.

DRAWER FRONTS

6"
1½"
1½"
4¾"
½"R.
5⅝"
3"
14⅝"

NOTCH 1" x 1" CENTER

BEVEL EDGES

13/16" TYP.

LARGE CENTRAL DRAWER ASSEMBLY

1¾"
1"
4"
2" O.C.
4⅞"

DOOR FOR HIDDEN COMPARTMENT CUT 2 FROM ¾" STOCK.

1½"
DRILL 1" DIA. FINGER HOLE
1½"
1⅛"
2½" O.C.
4¾"

SMALL DRAWER FRONT CUT 2 FROM ¾" STOCK.

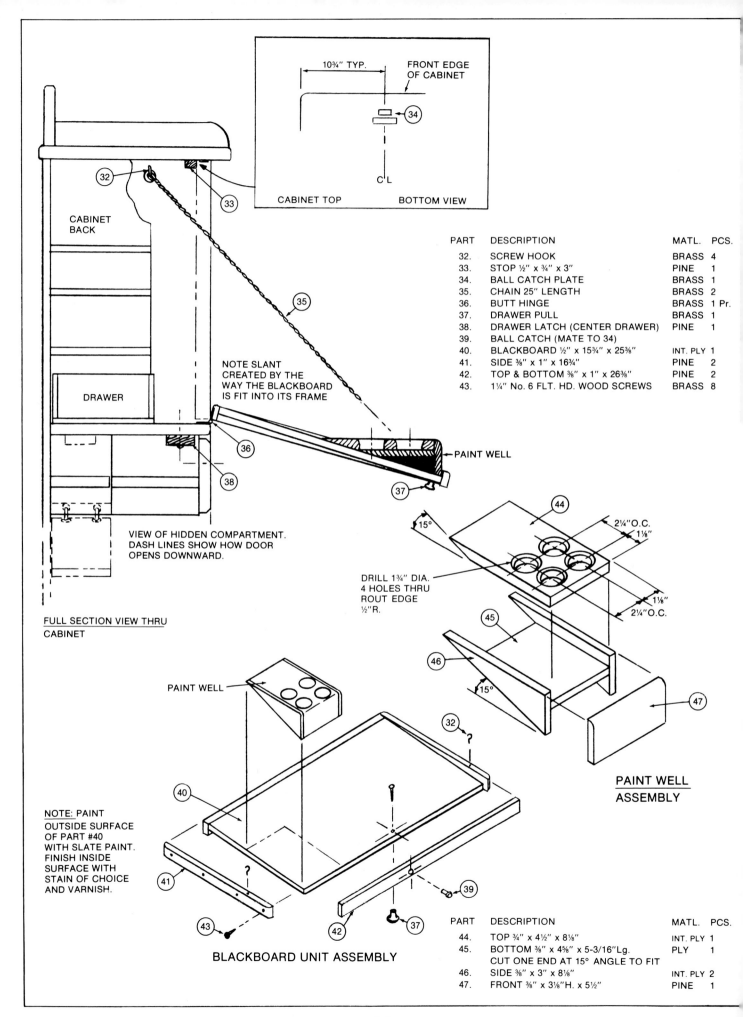

10¾" TYP.

FRONT EDGE OF CABINET

34

C L

CABINET TOP   BOTTOM VIEW

PART	DESCRIPTION	MATL.	PCS.
32.	SCREW HOOK	BRASS	4
33.	STOP ½" x ¾" x 3"	PINE	1
34.	BALL CATCH PLATE	BRASS	1
35.	CHAIN 25" LENGTH	BRASS	2
36.	BUTT HINGE	BRASS	1 Pr.
37.	DRAWER PULL	BRASS	1
38.	DRAWER LATCH (CENTER DRAWER)	PINE	1
39.	BALL CATCH (MATE TO 34)		
40.	BLACKBOARD ½" x 15¾" x 25⅜"	INT. PLY	1
41.	SIDE ⅜" x 1" x 16¾"	PINE	2
42.	TOP & BOTTOM ⅜" x 1" x 26⅜"	PINE	2
43.	1¼" No. 6 FLT. HD. WOOD SCREWS	BRASS	8

CABINET BACK

DRAWER

NOTE SLANT CREATED BY THE WAY THE BLACKBOARD IS FIT INTO ITS FRAME

PAINT WELL

DRILL 1¾" DIA. 4 HOLES THRU ROUT EDGE ½"R.

2¼"O.C.
1⅛"
1⅛"
2¼"O.C.

15°

15°

VIEW OF HIDDEN COMPARTMENT. DASH LINES SHOW HOW DOOR OPENS DOWNWARD.

FULL SECTION VIEW THRU CABINET

PAINT WELL

PAINT WELL ASSEMBLY

NOTE: PAINT OUTSIDE SURFACE OF PART #40 WITH SLATE PAINT. FINISH INSIDE SURFACE WITH STAIN OF CHOICE AND VARNISH.

BLACKBOARD UNIT ASSEMBLY

PART	DESCRIPTION	MATL.	PCS.
44.	TOP ¾" x 4½" x 8⅛"	INT. PLY	1
45.	BOTTOM ⅜" x 4⅝" x 5-3/16"Lg.	PLY	1
	CUT ONE END AT 15° ANGLE TO FIT		
46.	SIDE ⅜" x 3" x 8⅛"	INT. PLY	2
47.	FRONT ⅜" x 3⅛"H. x 5½"	PINE	1

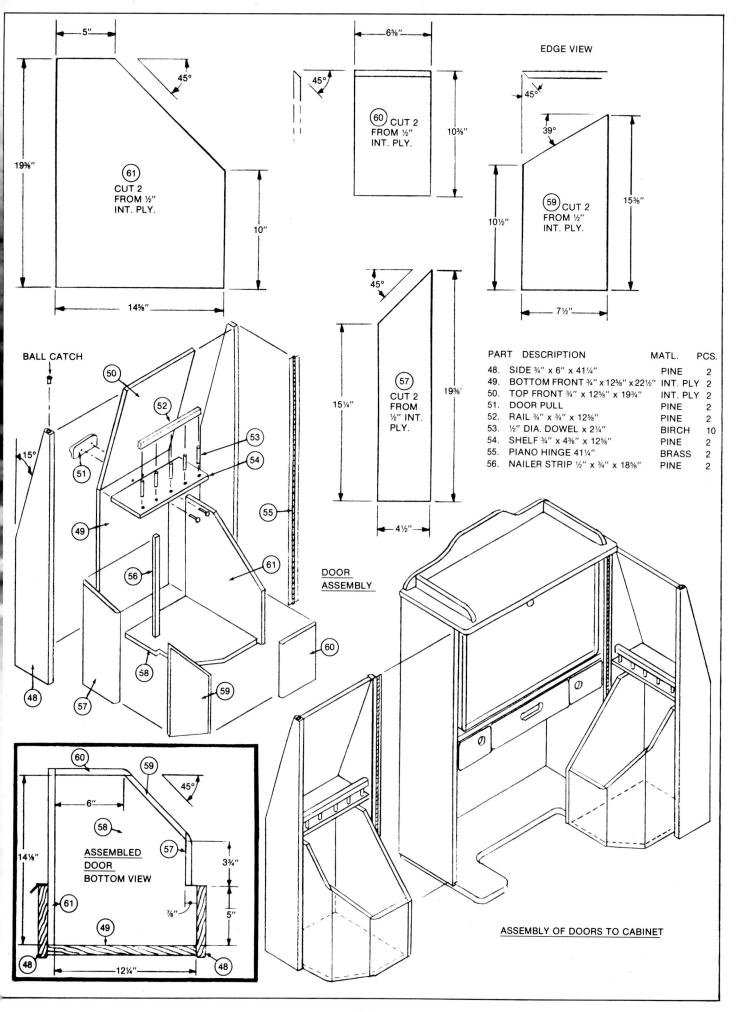

5"

45°

19⅜"

61 CUT 2 FROM ½" INT. PLY.

10"

14⅝"

6⅝"

45°

60 CUT 2 FROM ½" INT. PLY.

10⅜"

EDGE VIEW

45°

39°

59 CUT 2 FROM ½" INT. PLY.

10½"

15⅜"

7½"

45°

57 CUT 2 FROM ½" INT. PLY.

15¼"

19⅜"

4½"

BALL CATCH

50

52

53

54

51

15°

49

56

61

55

DOOR ASSEMBLY

58

48

57

59

60

PART	DESCRIPTION	MATL.	PCS.
48.	SIDE ¾" x 6" x 41¼"	PINE	2
49.	BOTTOM FRONT ¾" x 12⅝" x 22½"	INT. PLY	2
50.	TOP FRONT ¾" x 12⅝" x 19¾"	INT. PLY	2
51.	DOOR PULL	PINE	2
52.	RAIL ¾" x ¾" x 12⅝"	PINE	2
53.	½" DIA. DOWEL x 2¼"	BIRCH	10
54.	SHELF ¾" x 4⅜" x 12⅝"	PINE	2
55.	PIANO HINGE 41¼"	BRASS	2
56.	NAILER STRIP ½" x ¾" x 18⅝"	PINE	2

ASSEMBLY OF DOORS TO CABINET

60

59

45°

58

6"

14⅛"

57

3¾"

5"

⅞"

61

ASSEMBLED DOOR BOTTOM VIEW

49

48

12¼"

48

Heidi's Hutch

Where but in a fine china hutch would you keep your best dishes. This one, of course, has been matched to our table and chairs so you can have a complete dining room set. This hutch even has an easy to reach fine silverware drawer hidden just under the hinged front half of the top. In the cabinet below, you have plenty of room for all those kitchen extras. It is also sized to be used with our stove and ice-box.

Size: 25¹/₂″ wide
16¹/₈″ deep
45″ high

Trestle Table and Chairs

It's tea time, and what a delightful way to entertain your friends on your brand new furniture. Get your best table cloth, a little jar of wild flowers, your 3 best friends and who could ask for anything more. I'm sure your friends will rave about this very sturdy, easy-to-make trestle style table and chairs that has generations of use built into it. Our own daughter wished this had come along before she had already gone through 3 sets of metal and plastic. It is also sized for use with our stove, icebox, and hutch.

Size: Table: 25″ x 23¹/₃ top 19⁵/₈″ high

Chair: 29″ high 14″ wide 11¹/₂″ deep

Heidi's Hutch

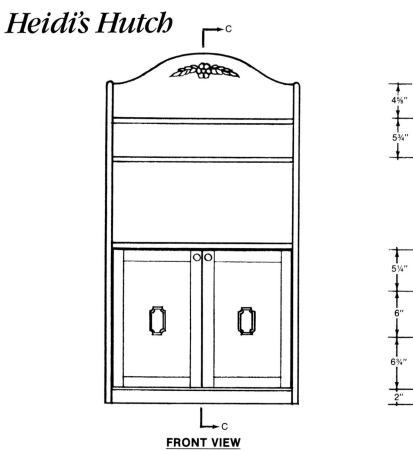

FRONT VIEW

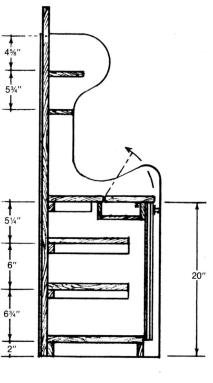

SIDE SECTION
SHOWS SHELF ALIGNMENT.
STUDY CAREFULLY

NOTE: IF PLYWOOD IS USED, ALLOW FOR ½" x ¾" WOOD GLUED, TO COVER EXPOSED PLYWOOD EDGES, GLUED-UP FIR IS AVAILABLE AT LUMBER STORES. BE SURE TO REVERSE GRAIN IF YOU ARE GLUING UP REGULAR PANELS.

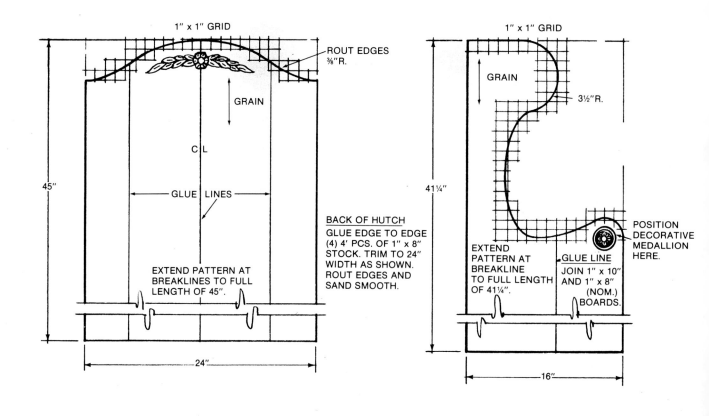

1" x 1" GRID

ROUT EDGES ⅜"R.

GRAIN

C L

GLUE LINES

45"

EXTEND PATTERN AT BREAKLINES TO FULL LENGTH OF 45".

24"

BACK OF HUTCH
GLUE EDGE TO EDGE (4) 4' PCS. OF 1" x 8" STOCK. TRIM TO 24" WIDTH AS SHOWN. ROUT EDGES AND SAND SMOOTH.

1" x 1" GRID

GRAIN

3½"R.

41¼"

EXTEND PATTERN AT BREAKLINE TO FULL LENGTH OF 41¼".

GLUE LINE
JOIN 1" x 10" AND 1" x 8" (NOM.) BOARDS.

POSITION DECORATIVE MEDALLION HERE.

16"

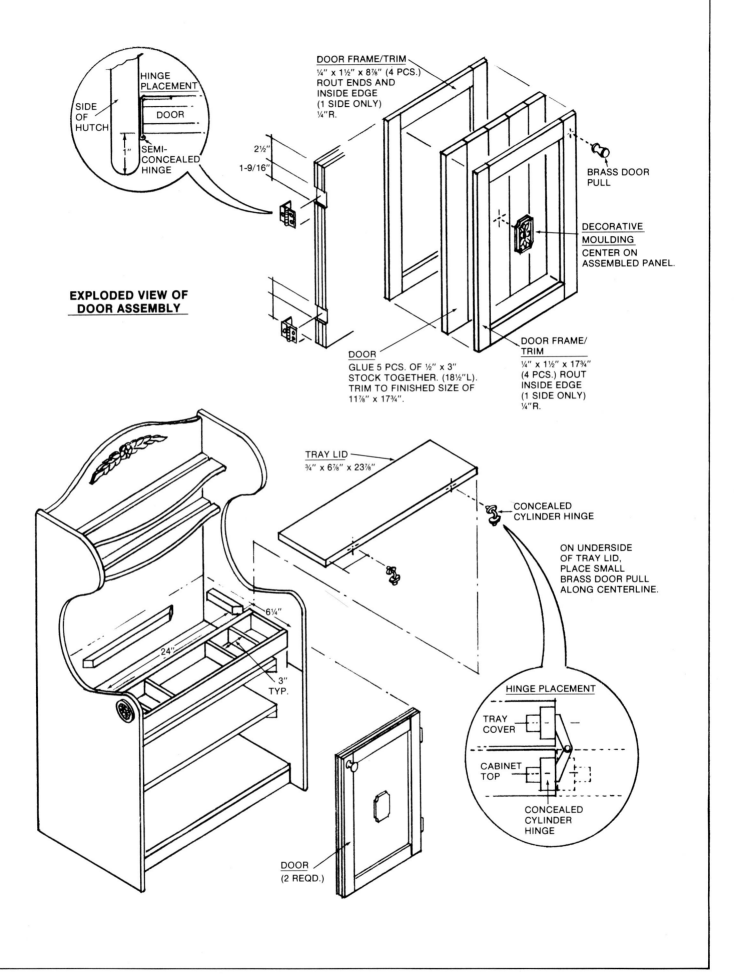

SIDE OF HUTCH

HINGE PLACEMENT

DOOR

SEMI-CONCEALED HINGE

1"

DOOR FRAME/TRIM
¼" x 1½" x 8⅞" (4 PCS.)
ROUT ENDS AND
INSIDE EDGE
(1 SIDE ONLY)
¼" R.

BRASS DOOR PULL

DECORATIVE MOULDING
CENTER ON
ASSEMBLED PANEL.

2½"

1-9/16"

EXPLODED VIEW OF DOOR ASSEMBLY

DOOR
GLUE 5 PCS. OF ½" x 3"
STOCK TOGETHER. (18½"L).
TRIM TO FINISHED SIZE OF
11⅞" x 17¾".

DOOR FRAME/ TRIM
¼" x 1½" x 17¾"
(4 PCS.) ROUT
INSIDE EDGE
(1 SIDE ONLY)
¼" R.

TRAY LID
¾" x 6⅞" x 23⅞"

CONCEALED CYLINDER HINGE

ON UNDERSIDE
OF TRAY LID,
PLACE SMALL
BRASS DOOR PULL
ALONG CENTERLINE.

6¼"

24"

3" TYP.

HINGE PLACEMENT

TRAY COVER

CABINET TOP

CONCEALED CYLINDER HINGE

DOOR
(2 REQD.)

PLATE GROOVES
CUT A 3/32" x ¼" DEEP DADO.
CUT 45° ANGLE, CLEAN AND SAND.

1" ⅞" 3/32"   3/32" ⅜" 1"

24"

PLATE
GROOVE

LOWER SHELF
CUT FROM 1" x 4" (NOM.)
24" LENGTH. ROUT
FRONT EDGES ⅛"R.

C̶L ̶

C̶L ̶

UPPER SHELF
CUT FROM 1" x 5" (NOM.)
STOCK, 24" LENGTH.
CUT GROOVE BEFORE
SHAPING FRONT.
ROUT FRONT EDGE
⅛"R.

**SIDE DECORATIVE
MEDALLION**
2¼" DIA. (2 REQD.)

**FRONT DOOR
DECORATION**
2"W. x 3¼"L.
(2 REQD.)

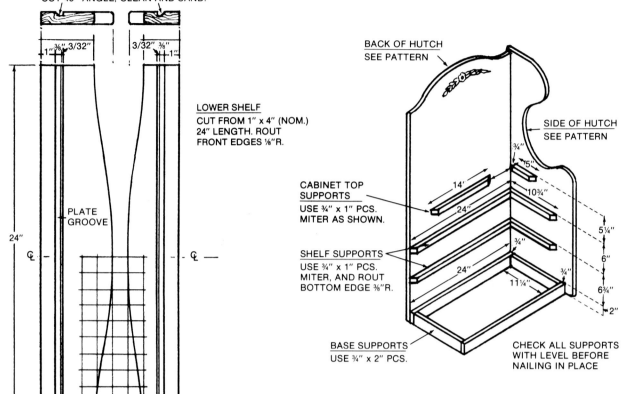

BACK OF HUTCH
SEE PATTERN

SIDE OF HUTCH
SEE PATTERN

**CABINET TOP
SUPPORTS**
USE ¾" x 1" PCS.
MITER AS SHOWN.

14"

24"

10¾"

¾"

5¼"

6"

6¾"

2"

SHELF SUPPORTS
USE ¾" x 1" PCS.
MITER, AND ROUT
BOTTOM EDGE ⅜"R.

24"

¾"

¾"

11¼"

BASE SUPPORTS
USE ¾" x 2" PCS.

CHECK ALL SUPPORTS
WITH LEVEL BEFORE
NAILING IN PLACE

AMT.	DESCRIPTION	MATL.	USE
2LF	1" x 5" (NOM.)	PINE	UPPER SHELF
4LF	1" x 4" (NOM.)	PINE	L. SHELF, SUPP.
30LF	1" x 8" (NOM.) FOR SHELVES, CAB. TOP, LID, SIDES, & BACK
8LF	1" x 10" (NOM.)	PINE	SIDES
4LF	1" x 12" (NOM.)	PINE	SHELVES
7LF	½" x 3" (NOM.)	PINE	UTENSIL TRAY
	6" x 24" ½" INTERIOR PLYWOOD	PINE	UTENSIL TRAY
8LF	1" x 3" (NOM.)	PINE	BASE SH. SUP.
2	DEC. MEDALLION	PINE	SIDES
1	DEC. MOULDING	PINE	FRONT
2	DEC. MOULDING	PINE	DOORS
2	CONCEALED HINGE	BRASS	TRAY LID
2PR.	SEMI-CONCEALED HINGE	BRASS	DOORS
2	REG. DRAWER KNOBS	BRASS	DOORS
1	SMALL DOOR PULL	BRASS	TRAY LID
16LF	¼" x 1½" LATTICE	PINE	DOOR TRIM

FINISHING NAILS, GLUE, STAIN, AND VARNISH AS NEEDED. ALLOW
10% CONSTRUCTION WASTE WHEN PURCHASING MATERIALS.

Trestle Table

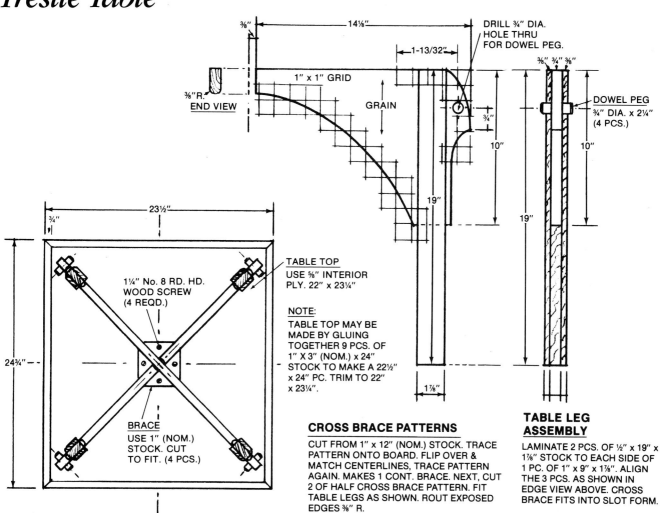

½"
⅜"R.
END VIEW

14⅛"

1" x 1" GRID
GRAIN

1-13/32"

DRILL ¾" DIA.
HOLE THRU
FOR DOWEL PEG.

¾"

10"

19"

19"

1⅞"

⅜" ¾" ⅜"

DOWEL PEG
¾" DIA. x 2¼"
(4 PCS.)

10"

**TABLE LEG
ASSEMBLY**

LAMINATE 2 PCS. OF ½" x 19" x
1⅞" STOCK TO EACH SIDE OF
1 PC. OF 1" x 9" x 1⅞". ALIGN
THE 3 PCS. AS SHOWN IN
EDGE VIEW ABOVE. CROSS
BRACE FITS INTO SLOT FORM.

23½"

¾"

24¾"

1¼" No. 8 RD. HD.
WOOD SCREW
(4 REQD.)

TABLE TOP
USE ⅝" INTERIOR
PLY. 22" x 23¼"

NOTE:
TABLE TOP MAY BE
MADE BY GLUING
TOGETHER 9 PCS. OF
1" X 3" (NOM.) x 24"
STOCK TO MAKE A 22½"
x 24" PC. TRIM TO 22"
x 23¼".

BRACE
USE 1" (NOM.)
STOCK. CUT
TO FIT. (4 PCS.)

TABLE ASSEMBLY

CROSS BRACE PATTERNS

CUT FROM 1" x 12" (NOM.) STOCK. TRACE
PATTERN ONTO BOARD. FLIP OVER &
MATCH CENTERLINES, TRACE PATTERN
AGAIN. MAKES 1 CONT. BRACE. NEXT, CUT
2 OF HALF CROSS BRACE PATTERN. FIT
TABLE LEGS AS SHOWN. ROUT EXPOSED
EDGES ⅜" R.

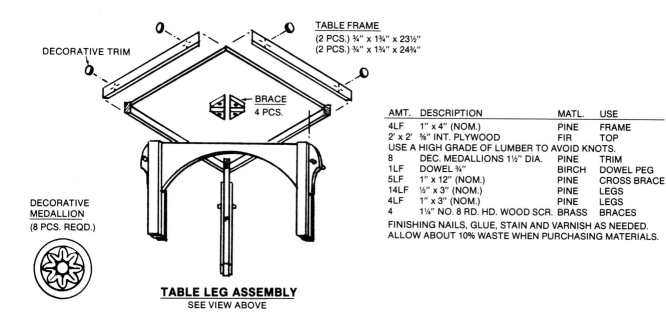

DECORATIVE TRIM

TABLE FRAME
(2 PCS.) ¾" x 1¾" x 23½"
(2 PCS.) ¾" x 1¾" x 24¾"

BRACE
4 PCS.

**DECORATIVE
MEDALLION**
(8 PCS. REQD.)

TABLE LEG ASSEMBLY
SEE VIEW ABOVE

AMT.	DESCRIPTION	MATL.	USE
4LF	1" x 4" (NOM.)	PINE	FRAME
2' x 2'	⅝" INT. PLYWOOD	FIR	TOP
USE A HIGH GRADE OF LUMBER TO AVOID KNOTS.			
8	DEC. MEDALLIONS 1½" DIA.	PINE	TRIM
1LF	DOWEL ¾"	BIRCH	DOWEL PEG
5LF	1" x 12" (NOM.)	PINE	CROSS BRACE
14LF	½" x 3" (NOM.)	PINE	LEGS
4LF	1" x 3" (NOM.)	PINE	LEGS
4	1¼" NO. 8 RD. HD. WOOD SCR.	BRASS	BRACES

FINISHING NAILS, GLUE, STAIN AND VARNISH AS NEEDED.
ALLOW ABOUT 10% WASTE WHEN PURCHASING MATERIALS.

Trestle Chair

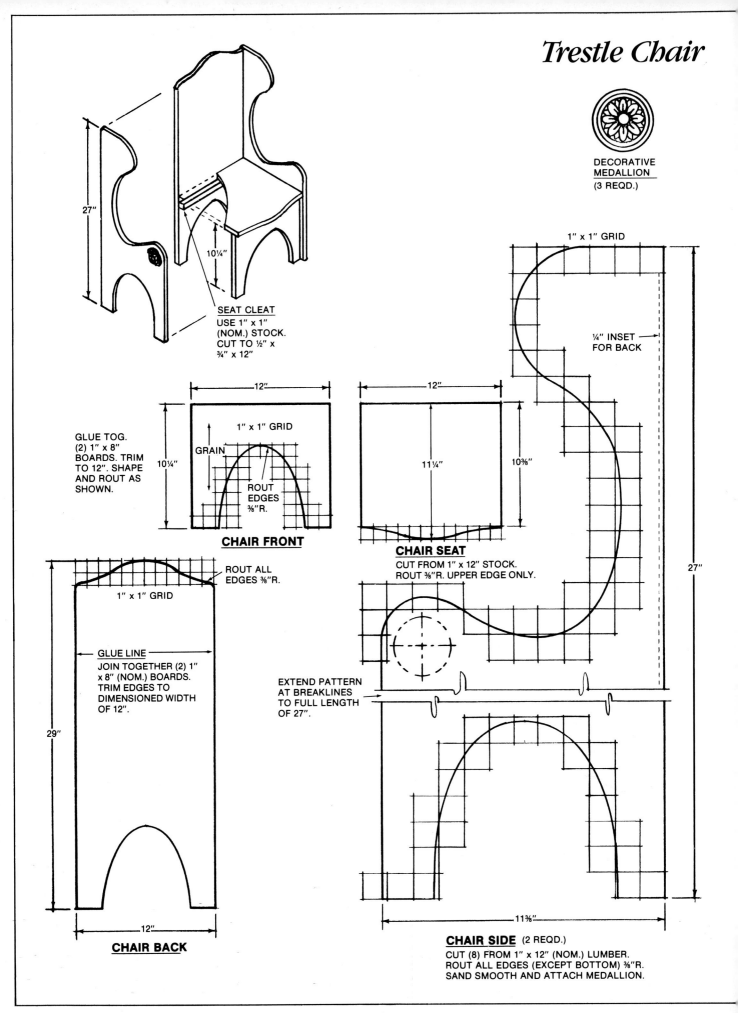

27"

10¼"

SEAT CLEAT
USE 1" x 1"
(NOM.) STOCK.
CUT TO ½" x
¾" x 12"

DECORATIVE MEDALLION
(3 REQD.)

1" x 1" GRID

¼" INSET
FOR BACK

27"

12"

GLUE TOG.
(2) 1" x 8"
BOARDS. TRIM
TO 12". SHAPE
AND ROUT AS
SHOWN.

1" x 1" GRID

GRAIN

10¼"

ROUT
EDGES
⅜"R.

CHAIR FRONT

12"

11¼"

10⅜"

CHAIR SEAT
CUT FROM 1" x 12" STOCK.
ROUT ⅜"R. UPPER EDGE ONLY.

ROUT ALL
EDGES ⅜"R.

1" x 1" GRID

GLUE LINE
JOIN TOGETHER (2) 1"
x 8" (NOM.) BOARDS.
TRIM EDGES TO
DIMENSIONED WIDTH
OF 12".

29"

EXTEND PATTERN
AT BREAKLINES
TO FULL LENGTH
OF 27".

12"

CHAIR BACK

11⅜"

CHAIR SIDE (2 REQD.)
CUT (8) FROM 1" x 12" (NOM.) LUMBER.
ROUT ALL EDGES (EXCEPT BOTTOM) ⅜"R.
SAND SMOOTH AND ATTACH MEDALLION.

Victoria

Truly an heir-loom! Any child would feel like royalty being pulled in this beautiful sleigh. Complete, comprehensive plans for all parts.

Size: 40" long without handle
20½" wide
25" high

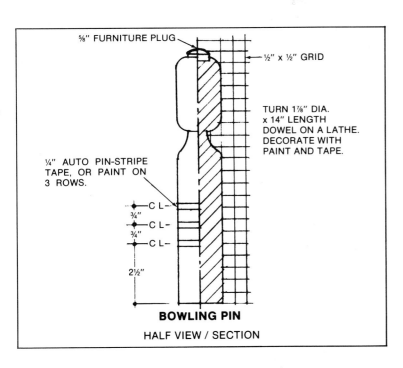

5⁄8" FURNITURE PLUG

1⁄2" x 1⁄2" GRID

TURN 1⁄8" DIA.
x 14" LENGTH
DOWEL ON A LATHE.
DECORATE WITH
PAINT AND TAPE.

1⁄4" AUTO PIN-STRIPE
TAPE, OR PAINT ON
3 ROWS.

C L—
3⁄4"
C L—
3⁄4"
C L—

2½"

BOWLING PIN

HALF VIEW / SECTION

Spare Time

If you're ever in doubt as to how to entertain your friends some evening, just bring out "Spare Time". A fun game for young and old. You can get the strikes, spares and splits just like downtown. Pins are easily turned on a lathe, and stripes are colored tape. A softball is the only other thing you need, and you're ready for fun.

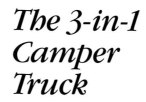

The 3-in-1 Camper Truck

A highly versatile and fun toy that will grow with the owner. Begins as a pick-up truck, with seat 9″ high. Advances to an old-time coal truck with 11″ seat. Then converts to a camper with the seat 13″ from the ground. Pickup and coal truck sections have enclosed, hinged compartments with plenty of room for carrying stones, sticks and frogs.

Size: 26″ long
10 ½″ wide
9″ high as pickup truck
11″ high as coal car
13″ high as camper
16″ to top of steering wheel

Tenbeards

Everyone delights in seeing these 10 little mountain men standing at attention, defying you to tip them over. Wait... don't think it's so easy, until you try it. Your bowling score will never be lower than with these smart little men.

Bunker Hill

A good sturdy traditional wood sled designed to give you many years of use. Turned wood grab rails are mounted on each side of this low, sleek beauty.

Size: 48¹/₂″ long
16″ wide
4″ high

The Family Circle

A game for the whole family. After dinner, treat Mom and Dad to a challenging game of Family Circle. Each family member is numbered, so it's easy to keep score. You can also move each person's arms up or down, depending on how difficult you want to make the game. People can be painted in the professions of your own family. Bottom also opens up to store people and hoop. Remember, the loser does dishes.

Size: 17¹⁄₈" wide
17³⁄₄" deep
16¹⁄₄" high

The Commander

A superior piece of equipment for loading and construction jobs. Crane boom moves forward and backward for a 29″ maximum breach. Breaks in the middle to pick up big jobs close to its base. When you've mastered the coordinations, you'll qualify as an engineer. A fascinating toy!

Size: 36¹/₂″ high
5¹/₂″ wide at
top of
platform
18″ wide at base

Turn-A-Pull

Here is an unusual wood action toy that will give hours of fun and will be a welcome addition to any construction fleet. It turns and maneuvers like the real thing. The pick-up opening can be finely adjusted, higher or lower, and be quickly dumped from the rear.

Size: 23¹/₂" long
       11¹/₂" wide
       10" high

Roadgrader

A good, sturdy wood toy whose front wheels turn with the steering wheel, and a grader blade that rotates 360°. Adjustable up and down for all your fine road work. Sized to use with all the other Ström construction toys.

Size: 22¹/₂" long
       8⁵/₈" wide
       8¹/₂" high

Roadgrader

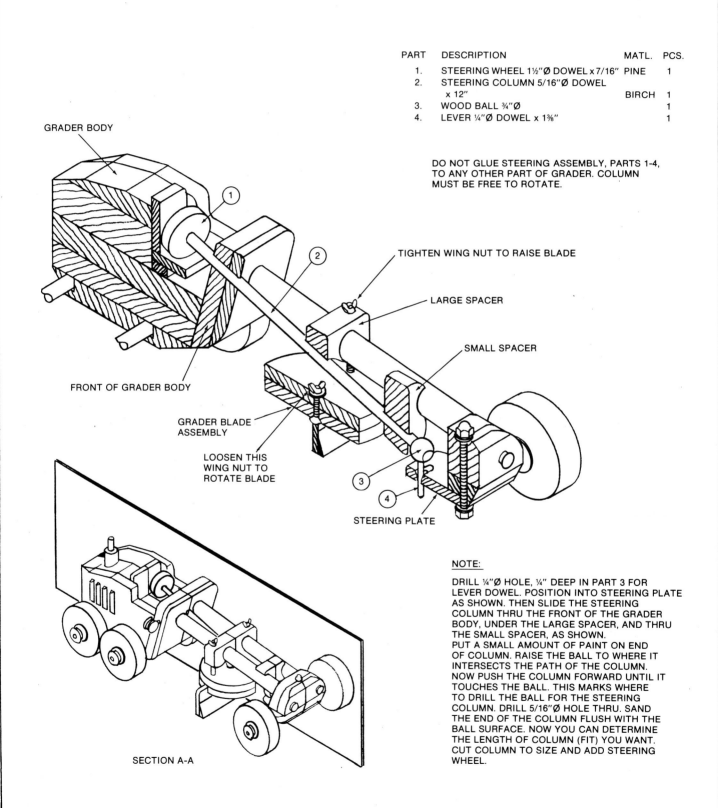

PART	DESCRIPTION	MATL.	PCS.
1.	STEERING WHEEL 1½"Ø DOWEL x 7/16"	PINE	1
2.	STEERING COLUMN 5/16"Ø DOWEL x 12"	BIRCH	1
3.	WOOD BALL ¾"Ø		1
4.	LEVER ¼"Ø DOWEL x 1⅜"		1

DO NOT GLUE STEERING ASSEMBLY, PARTS 1-4,
TO ANY OTHER PART OF GRADER. COLUMN
MUST BE FREE TO ROTATE.

GRADER BODY

FRONT OF GRADER BODY

GRADER BLADE
ASSEMBLY

LOOSEN THIS
WING NUT TO
ROTATE BLADE

TIGHTEN WING NUT TO RAISE BLADE

LARGE SPACER

SMALL SPACER

STEERING PLATE

SECTION A-A

NOTE:

DRILL ¼"Ø HOLE, ¼" DEEP IN PART 3 FOR
LEVER DOWEL. POSITION INTO STEERING PLATE
AS SHOWN. THEN SLIDE THE STEERING
COLUMN THRU THE FRONT OF THE GRADER
BODY, UNDER THE LARGE SPACER, AND THRU
THE SMALL SPACER, AS SHOWN.
PUT A SMALL AMOUNT OF PAINT ON END
OF COLUMN. RAISE THE BALL TO WHERE IT
INTERSECTS THE PATH OF THE COLUMN.
NOW PUSH THE COLUMN FORWARD UNTIL IT
TOUCHES THE BALL. THIS MARKS WHERE
TO DRILL THE BALL FOR THE STEERING
COLUMN. DRILL 5/16"Ø HOLE THRU. SAND
THE END OF THE COLUMN FLUSH WITH THE
BALL SURFACE. NOW YOU CAN DETERMINE
THE LENGTH OF COLUMN (FIT) YOU WANT.
CUT COLUMN TO SIZE AND ADD STEERING
WHEEL.

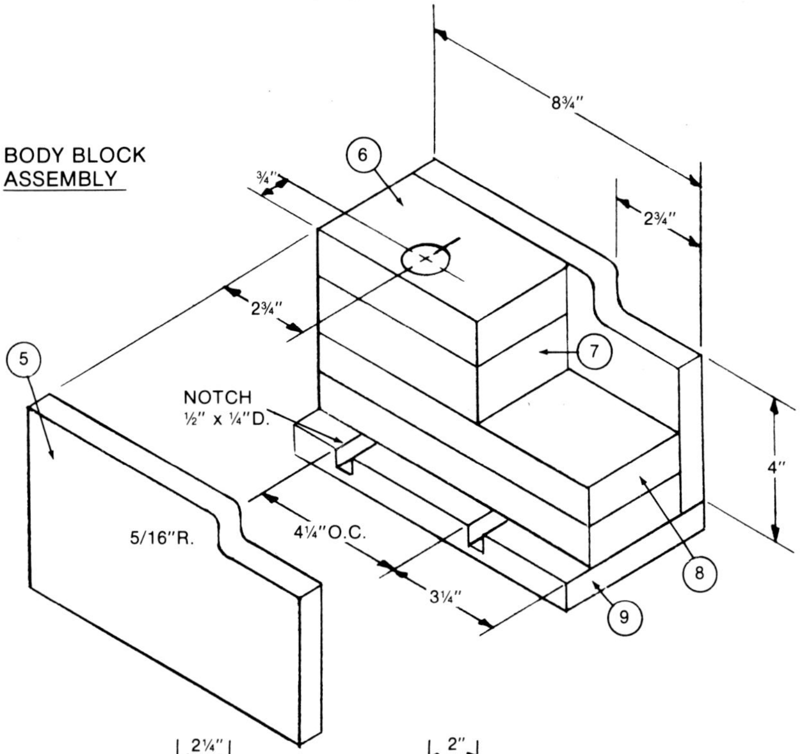

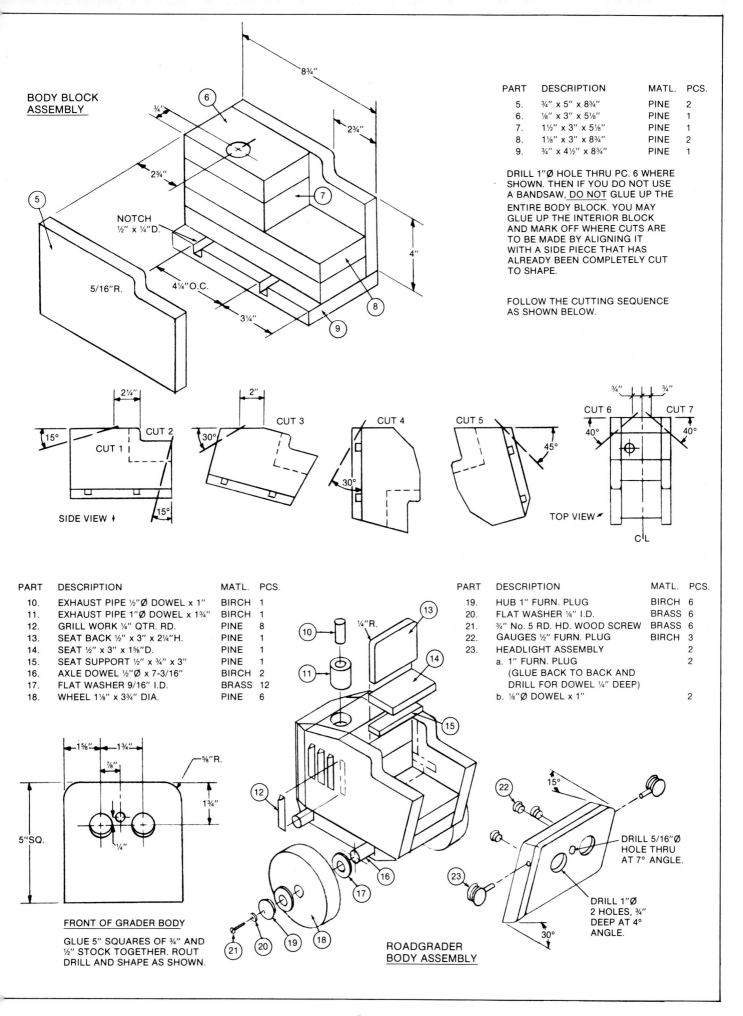

BODY BLOCK
ASSEMBLY
8¾″
¾″
6
2¾″
2¾″
7
5
NOTCH
½″ x ¼″D.
4″
5/16″R.
4¼″O.C.
8
3¼″
9

PART	DESCRIPTION	MATL.	PCS.
5.	¾″ x 5″ x 8¾″	PINE	2
6.	⅛″ x 3″ x 5⅛″	PINE	1
7.	1½″ x 3″ x 5⅛″	PINE	1
8.	1⅛″ x 3″ x 8¾″	PINE	2
9.	¾″ x 4½″ x 8¾″	PINE	1

DRILL 1″Ø HOLE THRU PC. 6 WHERE SHOWN. THEN IF YOU DO NOT USE A BANDSAW, DO NOT GLUE UP THE ENTIRE BODY BLOCK. YOU MAY GLUE UP THE INTERIOR BLOCK AND MARK OFF WHERE CUTS ARE TO BE MADE BY ALIGNING IT WITH A SIDE PIECE THAT HAS ALREADY BEEN COMPLETELY CUT TO SHAPE.

FOLLOW THE CUTTING SEQUENCE AS SHOWN BELOW.

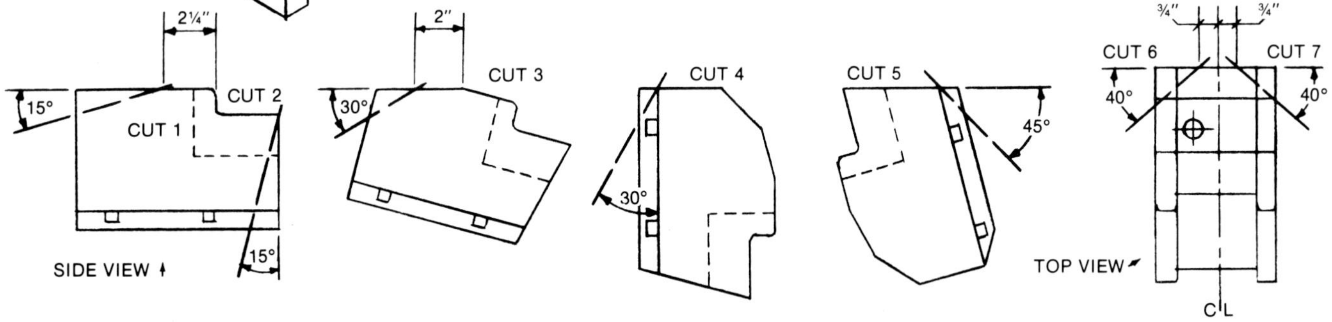

2¼″
15°
CUT 2
CUT 1
15°
SIDE VIEW
2″
CUT 3
30°
CUT 4
30°
CUT 5
45°
¾″
¾″
CUT 6
CUT 7
40°
40°
TOP VIEW
C L

PART	DESCRIPTION	MATL.	PCS.
10.	EXHAUST PIPE ½″Ø DOWEL x 1″	BIRCH	1
11.	EXHAUST PIPE 1″Ø DOWEL x 1¾″	BIRCH	1
12.	GRILL WORK ¼″ QTR. RD.	PINE	8
13.	SEAT BACK ½″ x 3″ x 2¼″H.	PINE	1
14.	SEAT ½″ x 3″ x 1⅝″D.	PINE	1
15.	SEAT SUPPORT ½″ x ¾″ x 3″	PINE	1
16.	AXLE DOWEL ½″Ø x 7-3/16″	BIRCH	2
17.	FLAT WASHER 9/16″ I.D.	BRASS	12
18.	WHEEL 1⅛″ x 3¾″ DIA.	PINE	6

PART	DESCRIPTION	MATL.	PCS.
19.	HUB 1″ FURN. PLUG	BIRCH	6
20.	FLAT WASHER ⅛″ I.D.	BRASS	6
21.	¾″ No. 5 RD. HD. WOOD SCREW	BRASS	6
22.	GAUGES ½″ FURN. PLUG	BIRCH	3
23.	HEADLIGHT ASSEMBLY		2
	a. 1″ FURN. PLUG (GLUE BACK TO BACK AND DRILL FOR DOWEL ¼″ DEEP)		2
	b. ⅛″Ø DOWEL x 1″		2

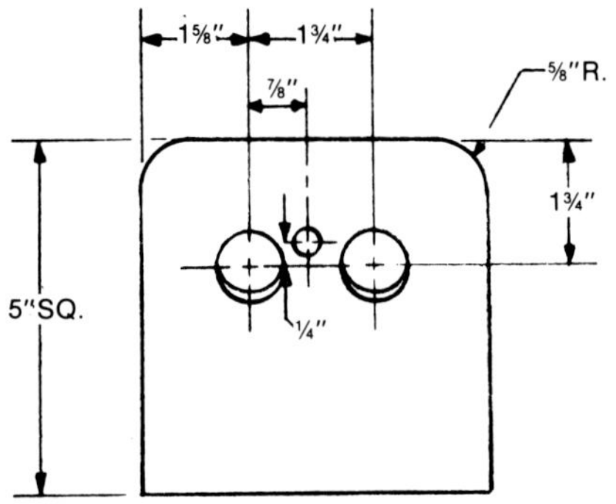

1⅝″
1¾″
⅞″
⅝″R.
1¾″
5″SQ.
¼″

FRONT OF GRADER BODY

GLUE 5″ SQUARES OF ¾″ AND ½″ STOCK TOGETHER. ROUT DRILL AND SHAPE AS SHOWN.

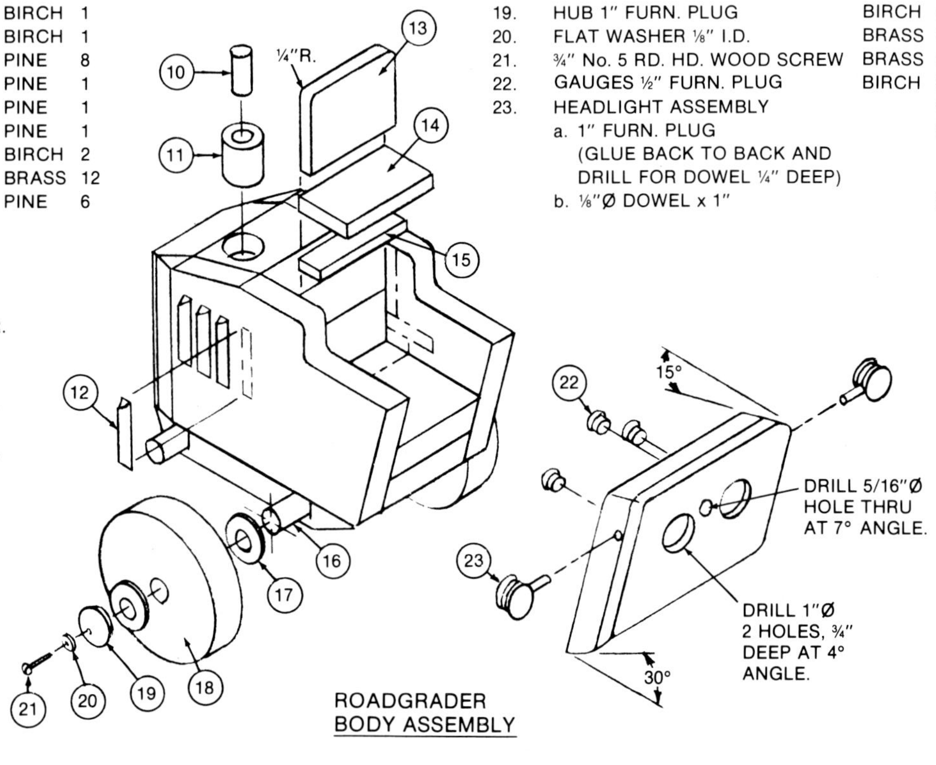

13
10
¼″R.
14
11
15
12
22
15°
DRILL 5/16″Ø
HOLE THRU
AT 7° ANGLE.
16
23
17
DRILL 1″Ø
2 HOLES, ¾″
DEEP AT 4°
ANGLE.
30°
18
19
20
21

ROADGRADER BODY ASSEMBLY

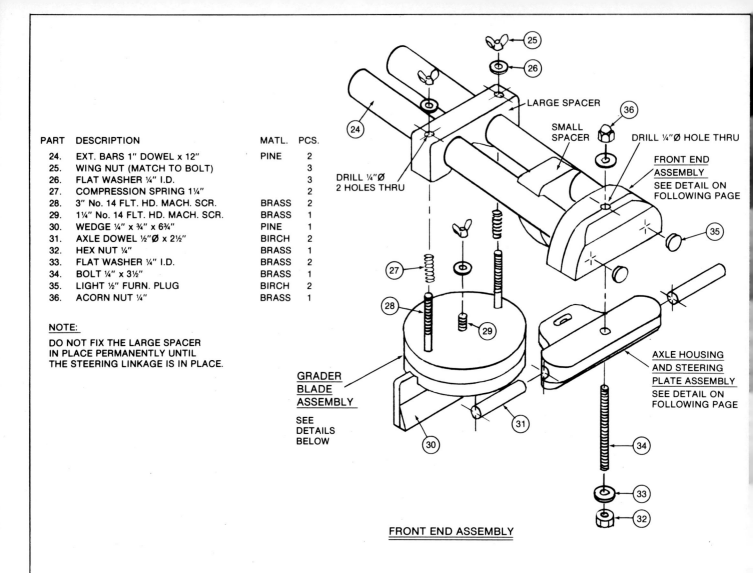

PART	DESCRIPTION	MATL.	PCS.
24.	EXT. BARS 1" DOWEL x 12"	PINE	2
25.	WING NUT (MATCH TO BOLT)		3
26.	FLAT WASHER ¼" I.D.		3
27.	COMPRESSION SPRING 1¼"		2
28.	3" No. 14 FLT. HD. MACH. SCR.	BRASS	2
29.	1¼" No. 14 FLT. HD. MACH. SCR.	BRASS	1
30.	WEDGE ¼" x ¾" x 6¾"	PINE	1
31.	AXLE DOWEL ½"Ø x 2½"	BIRCH	2
32.	HEX NUT ¼"	BRASS	1
33.	FLAT WASHER ¼" I.D.	BRASS	2
34.	BOLT ¼" x 3½"	BRASS	1
35.	LIGHT ½" FURN. PLUG	BIRCH	2
36.	ACORN NUT ¼"	BRASS	1

NOTE:

DO NOT FIX THE LARGE SPACER IN PLACE PERMANENTLY UNTIL THE STEERING LINKAGE IS IN PLACE.

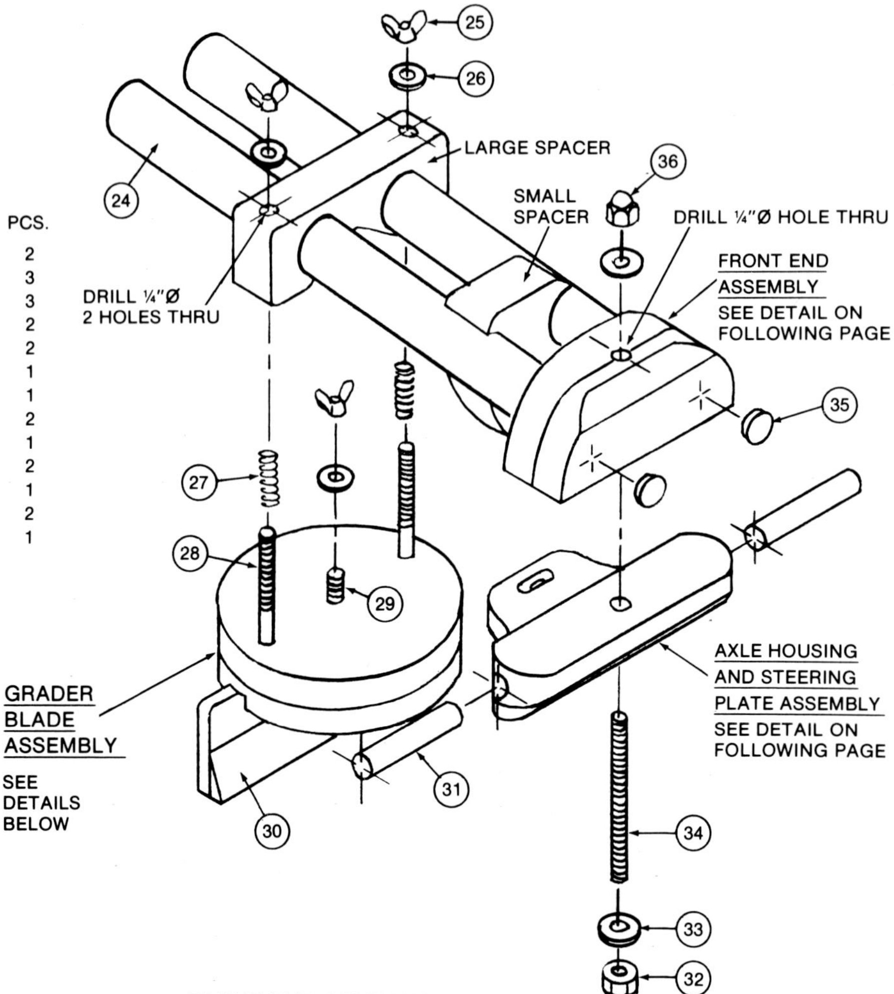
25
26
LARGE SPACER
36
24
SMALL SPACER
DRILL ¼"Ø HOLE THRU
FRONT END ASSEMBLY
SEE DETAIL ON FOLLOWING PAGE
DRILL ¼"Ø 2 HOLES THRU
35
27
28
29
AXLE HOUSING AND STEERING PLATE ASSEMBLY
SEE DETAIL ON FOLLOWING PAGE
GRADER BLADE ASSEMBLY
SEE DETAILS BELOW
31
30
34
33
32

FRONT END ASSEMBLY

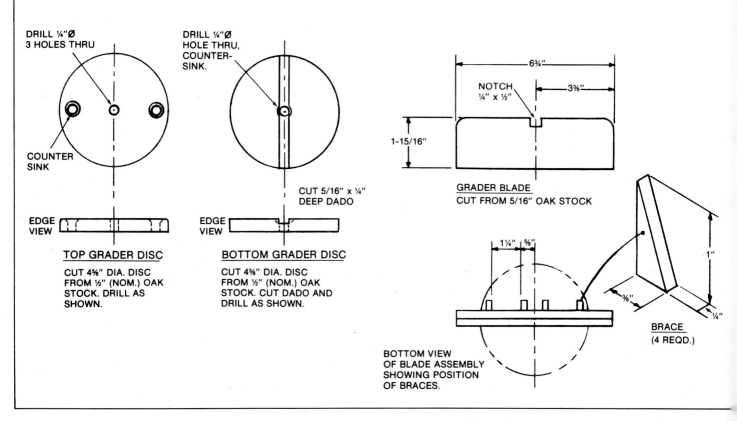

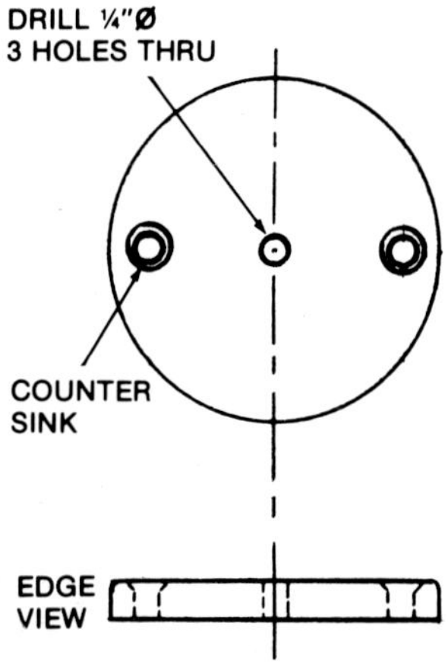
DRILL ¼"Ø 3 HOLES THRU
COUNTER SINK
EDGE VIEW

TOP GRADER DISC

CUT 4⅝" DIA. DISC FROM ½" (NOM.) OAK STOCK. DRILL AS SHOWN.

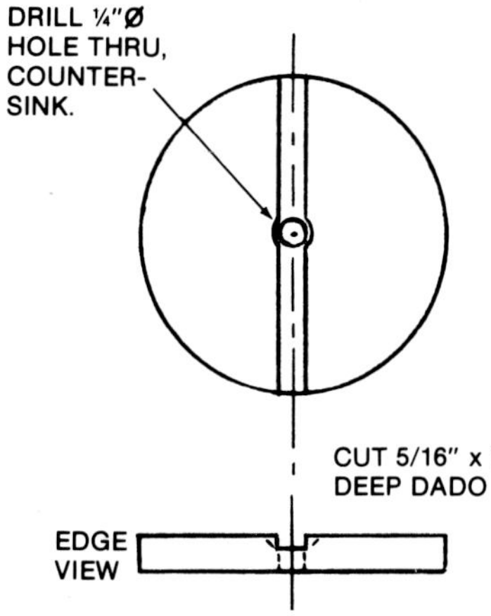
DRILL ¼"Ø HOLE THRU, COUNTER-SINK.
CUT 5/16" x ¼" DEEP DADO
EDGE VIEW

BOTTOM GRADER DISC

CUT 4⅝" DIA. DISC FROM ½" (NOM.) OAK STOCK. CUT DADO AND DRILL AS SHOWN.

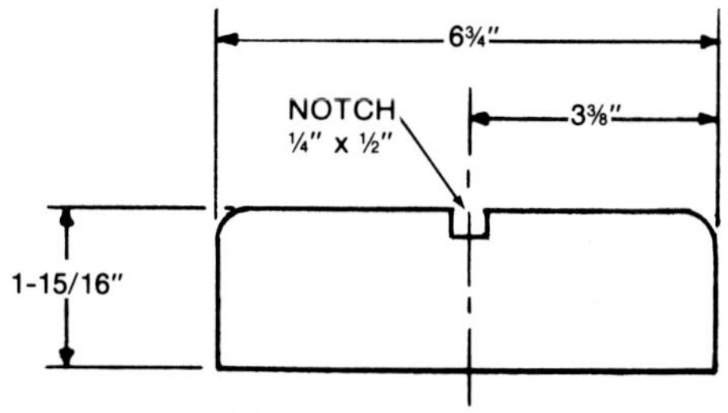
6¾"
NOTCH ¼" x ½"
3⅜"
1-15/16"

GRADER BLADE

CUT FROM 5/16" OAK STOCK

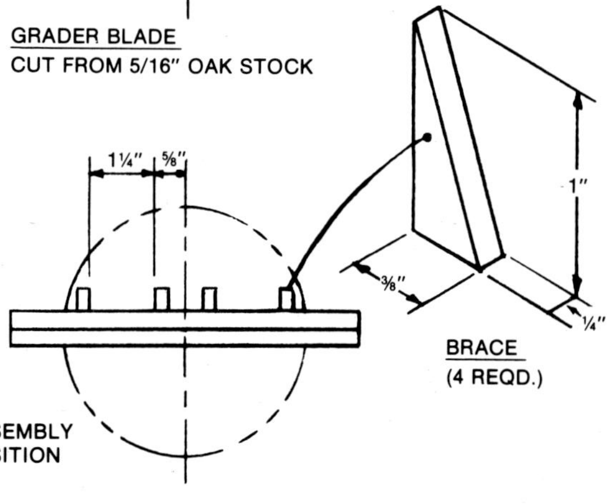
1¼"
⅝"
1"
⅜"
¼"

BOTTOM VIEW OF BLADE ASSEMBLY SHOWING POSITION OF BRACES.

BRACE

(4 REQD.)

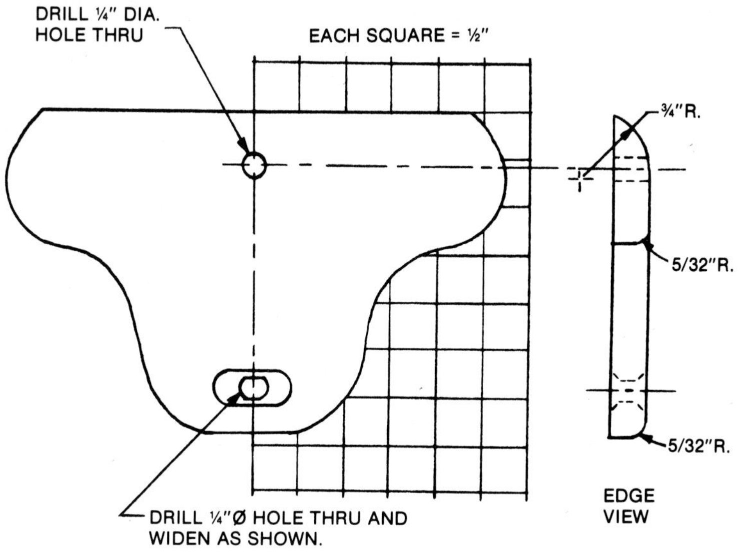
DRILL ¼" DIA. HOLE THRU
EACH SQUARE = ½"
¾"R.
5/32"R.
5/32"R.
EDGE VIEW
DRILL ¼"Ø HOLE THRU AND WIDEN AS SHOWN.

STEERING PLATE

CUT FROM ½" (NOM.) OAK STOCK.

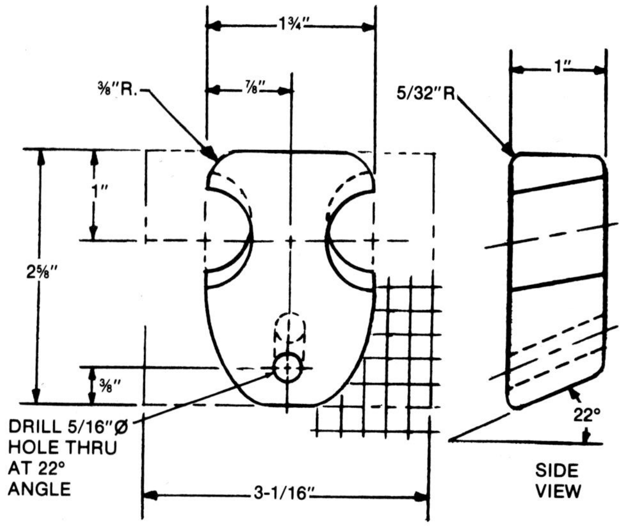
1¾"
⅞"
⅜"R.
1"
2⅝"
⅜"
DRILL 5/16"Ø HOLE THRU AT 22° ANGLE
3-1/16"
1"
5/32"R.
22°
SIDE VIEW

SMALL SPACER

GLUE TOGETHER 2 PCS. ½" (NOM.) OAK STOCK. EACH SQUARE = ¼"

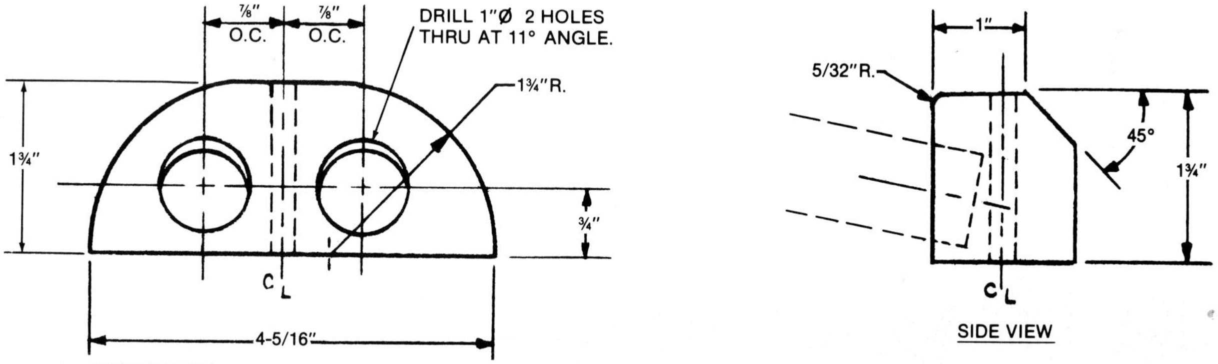
⅞" O.C.
⅞" O.C.
DRILL 1"Ø 2 HOLES THRU AT 11° ANGLE.
1¾"R.
1¾"
¾"
CL
4-5/16"
1"
5/32"R.
45°
1¾"
CL
SIDE VIEW

FRONT END

GLUE 2 PCS. OF 1" (NOM.) STOCK TOGETHER.

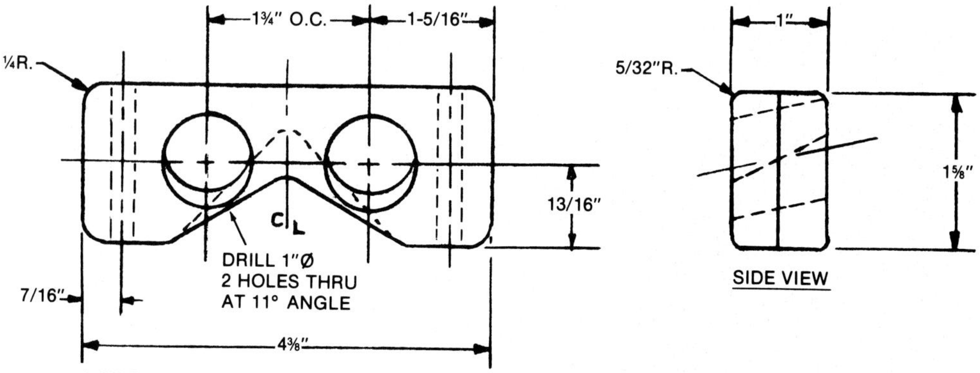
1¾" O.C.
1-5/16"
¼R.
CL
13/16"
DRILL 1"Ø 2 HOLES THRU AT 11° ANGLE
7/16"
4⅜"
1"
5/32"R.
1⅝"
SIDE VIEW

LARGE SPACER

GLUE 2 PCS. OF ½" (NOM.) STOCK TOGETHER, CUT OUT WEDGE SHAPED RECESS FOR STEERING LINKAGE.

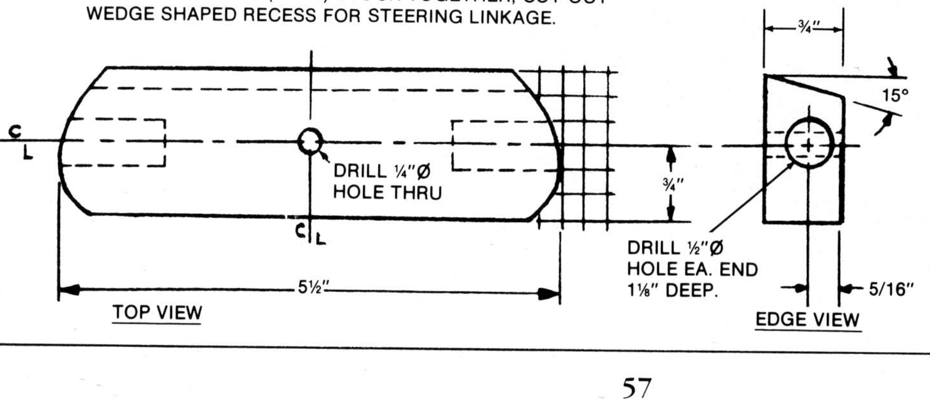
CL
DRILL ¼"Ø HOLE THRU
CL
¾"
5½"
TOP VIEW
¾"
15°
DRILL ½"Ø HOLE EA. END 1⅛" DEEP.
5/16"
EDGE VIEW

FRONT AXLE HOUSING

CUT AND SHAPE FROM 1" x 2" (NOM.) STOCK.
EACH SQUARE = ¼"

Sparky

A special riding horse for young-er children that rides and turns easily, and doesn't need much room for maneuvering.

Size: **22" long**
9½" wide
Seat—11" high
Head—16" high

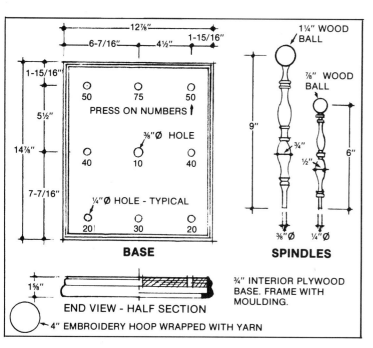

BASE

12⅞"
6-7/16"
4½"
1-15/16"

1-15/16"

5½"

14⅞"

7-7/16"

50 75 50

PRESS ON NUMBERS

⅜"Ø HOLE

40 10 40

¼"Ø HOLE - TYPICAL

20 30 20

SPINDLES

1¼" WOOD BALL

⅞" WOOD BALL

9"

¾"

½"

6"

⅜"Ø   ¼"Ø

1⅝"

END VIEW - HALF SECTION

¾" INTERIOR PLYWOOD BASE. FRAME WITH MOULDING.

4" EMBROIDERY HOOP WRAPPED WITH YARN

Roundabout

A ring toss game made from furniture spindles and balls that will provide many hours of competition and enjoyment. Easy to make . . . but that 75 is a tough score to hit.

**Size: 12¾" wide
14⅞" deep
10" high**

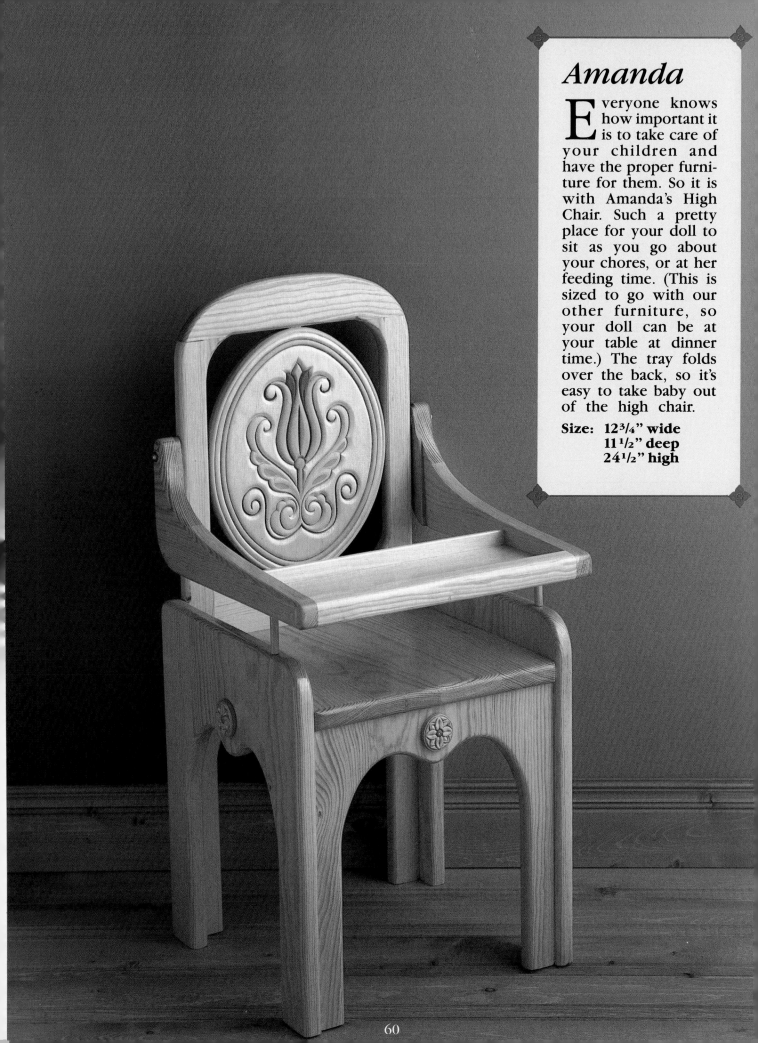

Amanda

Everyone knows how important it is to take care of your children and have the proper furniture for them. So it is with Amanda's High Chair. Such a pretty place for your doll to sit as you go about your chores, or at her feeding time. (This is sized to go with our other furniture, so your doll can be at your table at dinner time.) The tray folds over the back, so it's easy to take baby out of the high chair.

Size: 12¾" wide
11½" deep
24½" high

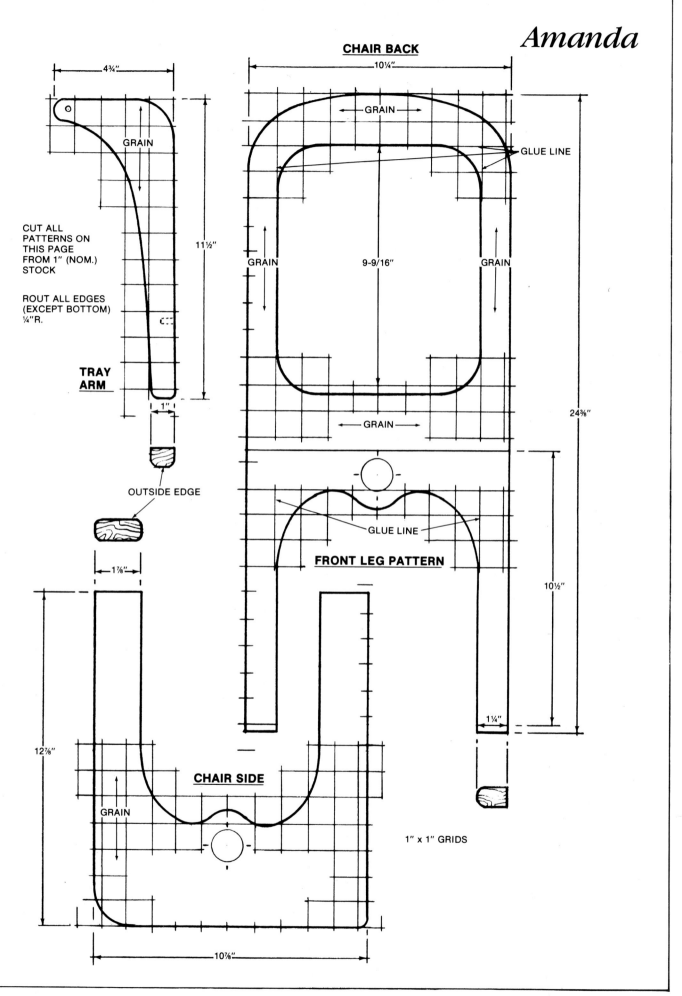

Amanda

CHAIR BACK

10¼"

GRAIN

GLUE LINE

GRAIN

9-9/16"

GRAIN

GRAIN

24⅜"

4¾"

GRAIN

CUT ALL
PATTERNS ON
THIS PAGE
FROM 1" (NOM.)
STOCK

ROUT ALL EDGES
(EXCEPT BOTTOM)
¼"R.

11½"

**TRAY
ARM**

1"

OUTSIDE EDGE

GLUE LINE

FRONT LEG PATTERN

10½"

1¼"

1⅞"

12⅞"

CHAIR SIDE

GRAIN

1" x 1" GRIDS

10⅞"

61

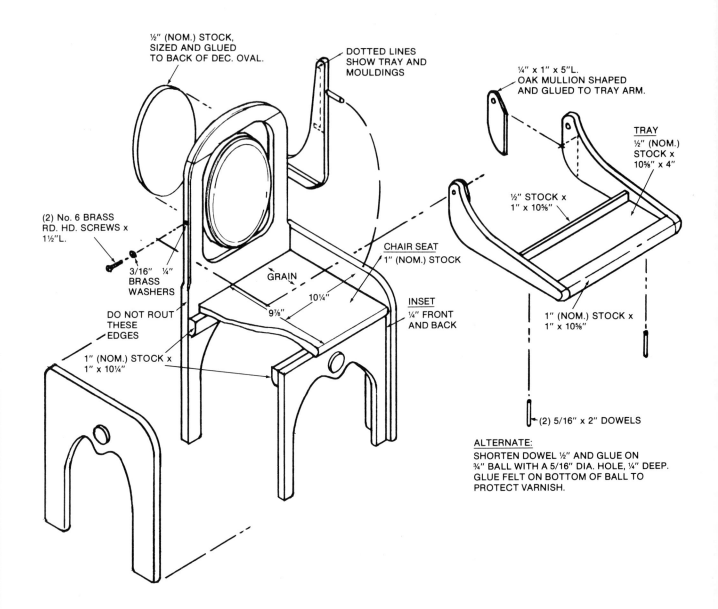

½" (NOM.) STOCK, SIZED AND GLUED TO BACK OF DEC. OVAL.

DOTTED LINES SHOW TRAY AND MOULDINGS

¼" x 1" x 5"L. OAK MULLION SHAPED AND GLUED TO TRAY ARM.

TRAY
½" (NOM.) STOCK x 10⅝" x 4"

(2) No. 6 BRASS RD. HD. SCREWS x 1½"L.

½" STOCK x 1" x 10⅝"

3/16" ¼" BRASS WASHERS

CHAIR SEAT
1" (NOM.) STOCK

GRAIN

DO NOT ROUT THESE EDGES

10¼"

9⅞"

INSET
¼" FRONT AND BACK

1" (NOM.) STOCK x 1" x 10⅝"

1" (NOM.) STOCK x 1" x 10¼"

(2) 5/16" x 2" DOWELS

ALTERNATE:
SHORTEN DOWEL ½" AND GLUE ON ¾" BALL WITH A 5/16" DIA. HOLE, ¼" DEEP. GLUE FELT ON BOTTOM OF BALL TO PROTECT VARNISH.

NOTES:
PRECUT, SAND AND TEMPORARILY TACK ALL PCS. TOGETHER FOR PROPER FIT BEFORE FINAL GLUING AND ASSEMBLY.

DECORATIVE ROSETTE AND BACK OVAL MAY BE AVAILABLE LOCALLY, FROM NATIONAL CATALOG SOURCES, OR MAY BE ORDERED AS AN ACCESSORY PACKAGE FROM SUN DESIGNS.

YOU MAY WISH TO PUT FELT ON BOTTOM OF DOWEL OR BALL, TO PROTECT VARNISH.

CHAIR BACK CAN BE MADE FROM ONE PIECE OR GLUED TOGETHER AS INDICATED.

DECORATIVE OVAL
9-9/16" x 7-13/16"

DECORATIVE MEDALLION
1-5/16" DIA.

Abigail

What a nice resting place for your favorite doll. Surely something to be treasured and passed on to the next generations. Has a nice, gentle motion. Plans include pattern for pad and pretty round pillow.

Size: 25″ long
13½″ wide, box only
24″ wide, with rockers
22″ high

Stake Wagon

A large wagon with interlocking stake sides that do not require hardware. Easily used with or without sides. Plans included for conversion to sleigh, making this a winter and summer wagon.

Size: 38″ long, box only
 19″ wide
 22″ high

Yankee Clipper

A good, old-fashioned sled like Grandpa used to ride on! Just wax the runners and away you go...

Size: 44″ long
14 ¹/₂″ wide
4 ³/₄″ high

Yankee Clipper

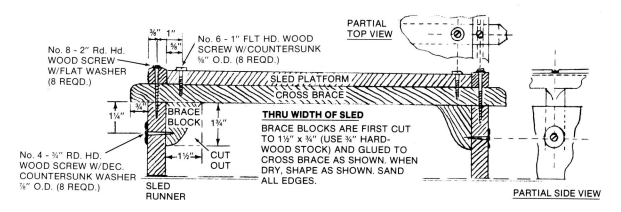

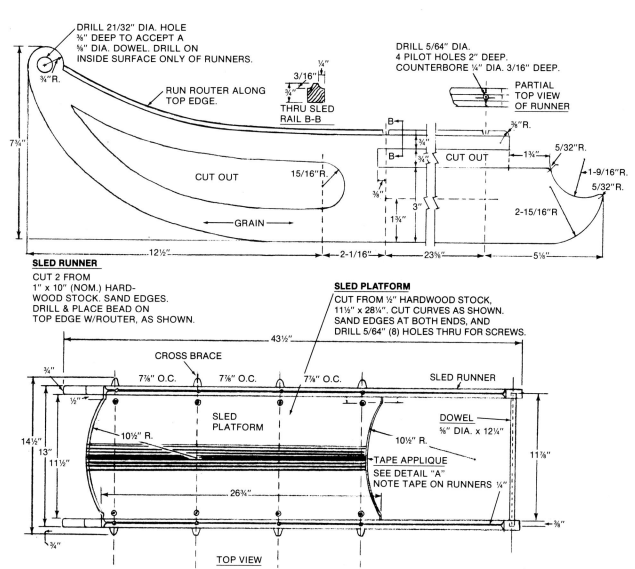

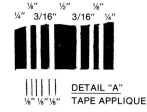

DETAIL "A"
TAPE APPLIQUE

Hard Rock Mining Company

This is a real neat action toy. Because of the size of this toy, and using sand, we recommend it be used outside. This has a continual motion—the buckets scoop up the sand and dump it down the chute into the loading car. When the car is full, the weight sends it down and dumps the sand into the bottom hopper. Weights in the box make the car go back to the loading position again. Turn the crank, and it starts all over again. This could keep someone *very* busy!

Size: **21¹/₂″ wide**
39¹/₄″ deep
29″ high

Box and Blocks

A great set of big blocks that can also be used as boxes. The largest box has wheels and a rope for pulling toys to where the action is.

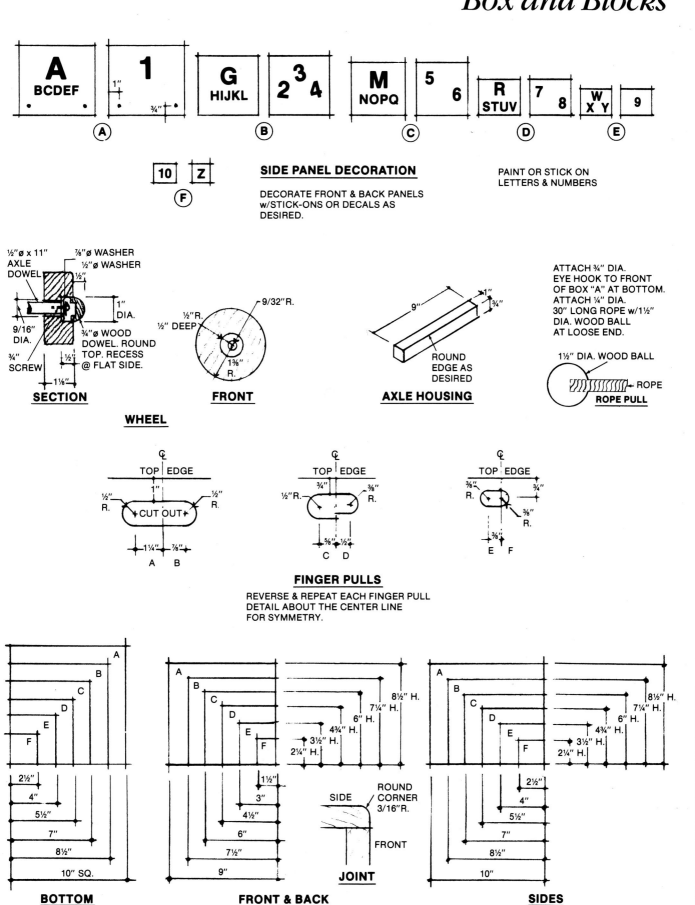

A BCDEF | **1** 1" ¾" | **G** HIJKL | **2** **3** **4**

Ⓐ | Ⓑ

M NOPQ | **5** **6** | **R** STUV | **7** **8** | **W** X Y | **9**

Ⓒ | Ⓓ | Ⓔ

10 **Z**

Ⓕ

SIDE PANEL DECORATION

DECORATE FRONT & BACK PANELS w/STICK-ONS OR DECALS AS DESIRED.

PAINT OR STICK ON LETTERS & NUMBERS

½"ø x 11" AXLE DOWEL
⅞"ø WASHER
½"ø WASHER
½"
1" DIA.
9/16" DIA.
¾"ø WOOD DOWEL. ROUND TOP. RECESS @ FLAT SIDE.
¾" SCREW
½"
1⅛"

SECTION

WHEEL

½"R. ½" DEEP
9/32"R.
1⅜" R.

FRONT

ATTACH ¾" DIA. EYE HOOK TO FRONT OF BOX "A" AT BOTTOM. ATTACH ¼" DIA. 30" LONG ROPE w/1½" DIA. WOOD BALL AT LOOSE END.

9" 1" ¾"
ROUND EDGE AS DESIRED

AXLE HOUSING

1½" DIA. WOOD BALL
ROPE

ROPE PULL

TOP EDGE
½" R.
1"
½" R.
CUT OUT
1¼" ⅞"
A B

TOP EDGE
¾"
½"R. ⅜" R.
⅝" ½"
C D

TOP EDGE
⅜" R.
¾"
⅜" R.
⅜"
E F

FINGER PULLS

REVERSE & REPEAT EACH FINGER PULL DETAIL ABOUT THE CENTER LINE FOR SYMMETRY.

A B C D E F
2½" 4" 5½" 7" 8½" 10" SQ.

BOTTOM
1 EACH

A B C D E F
8½" H. 7¼" H. 6" H. 4¾" H. 3½" H. 2¼" H.
1½" 3" 4½" 6" 7½" 9"

SIDE
ROUND CORNER 3/16"R.
FRONT

JOINT

FRONT & BACK
2 EACH

A B C D E F
8½" H. 7¼" H. 6" H. 4¾" H. 3½" H. 2¼" H.
2½" 4" 5½" 7" 8½" 10"

SIDES
2 EACH

Swedish Sled

A type of sled used in Sweden for many generations; to haul the children, bring in the wood or carry the groceries. Can be pushed or pulled. A truly one-of-a-kind design.

Size: 33″ long to top of handle
6″ high, box only
19″ wide
30½″ long

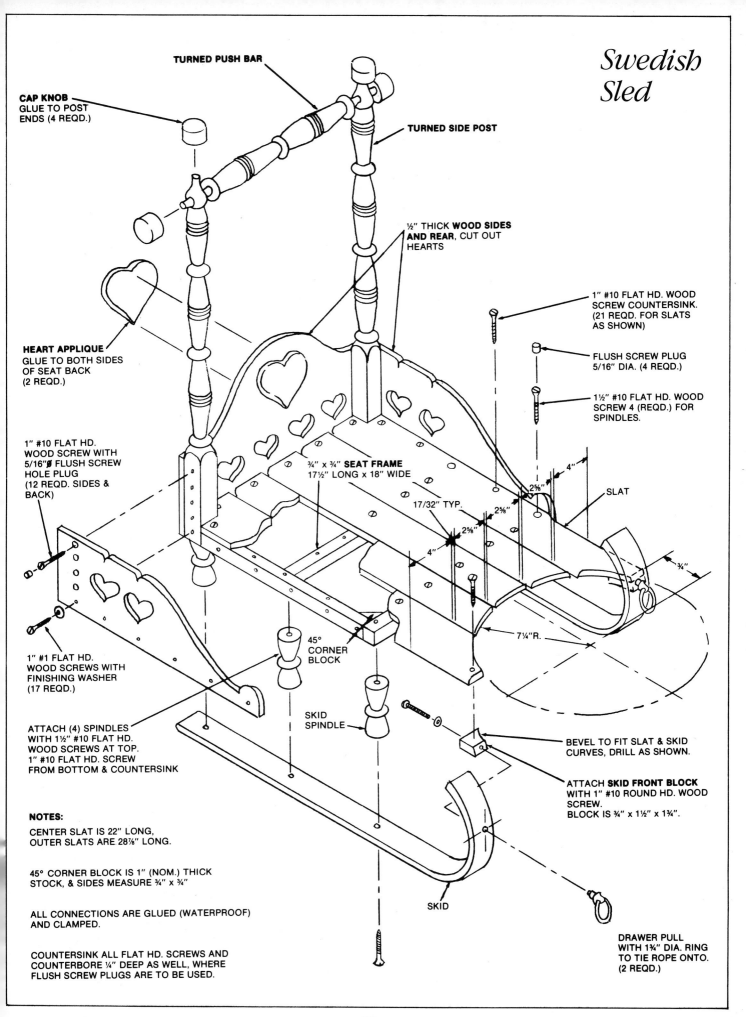

TURNED PUSH BAR

CAP KNOB
GLUE TO POST
ENDS (4 REQD.)

TURNED SIDE POST

½" THICK **WOOD SIDES AND REAR**, CUT OUT HEARTS

1" #10 FLAT HD. WOOD
SCREW COUNTERSINK.
(21 REQD. FOR SLATS
AS SHOWN)

FLUSH SCREW PLUG
5/16" DIA. (4 REQD.)

1½" #10 FLAT HD. WOOD
SCREW 4 (REQD.) FOR
SPINDLES.

HEART APPLIQUE
GLUE TO BOTH SIDES
OF SEAT BACK
(2 REQD.)

1" #10 FLAT HD.
WOOD SCREW WITH
5/16"Ø FLUSH SCREW
HOLE PLUG
(12 REQD. SIDES &
BACK)

¾" x ¾" **SEAT FRAME**
17½" LONG x 18" WIDE

17/32" TYP.

2⅝"

2⅝"

2⅝"

4"

4"

SLAT

¾"

7¼"R.

45°
CORNER
BLOCK

1" #1 FLAT HD.
WOOD SCREWS WITH
FINISHING WASHER
(17 REQD.)

SKID
SPINDLE

ATTACH (4) SPINDLES
WITH 1½" #10 FLAT HD.
WOOD SCREWS AT TOP.
1" #10 FLAT HD. SCREW
FROM BOTTOM & COUNTERSINK

BEVEL TO FIT SLAT & SKID
CURVES, DRILL AS SHOWN.

ATTACH **SKID FRONT BLOCK**
WITH 1" #10 ROUND HD. WOOD
SCREW.
BLOCK IS ¾" x 1½" x 1¾".

SKID

NOTES:

CENTER SLAT IS 22" LONG,
OUTER SLATS ARE 28⅞" LONG.

45° CORNER BLOCK IS 1" (NOM.) THICK
STOCK, & SIDES MEASURE ¾" x ¾"

ALL CONNECTIONS ARE GLUED (WATERPROOF)
AND CLAMPED.

COUNTERSINK ALL FLAT HD. SCREWS AND
COUNTERBORE ¼" DEEP AS WELL, WHERE
FLUSH SCREW PLUGS ARE TO BE USED.

DRAWER PULL
WITH 1¾" DIA. RING
TO TIE ROPE ONTO.
(2 REQD.)

*Swedish
Sled*

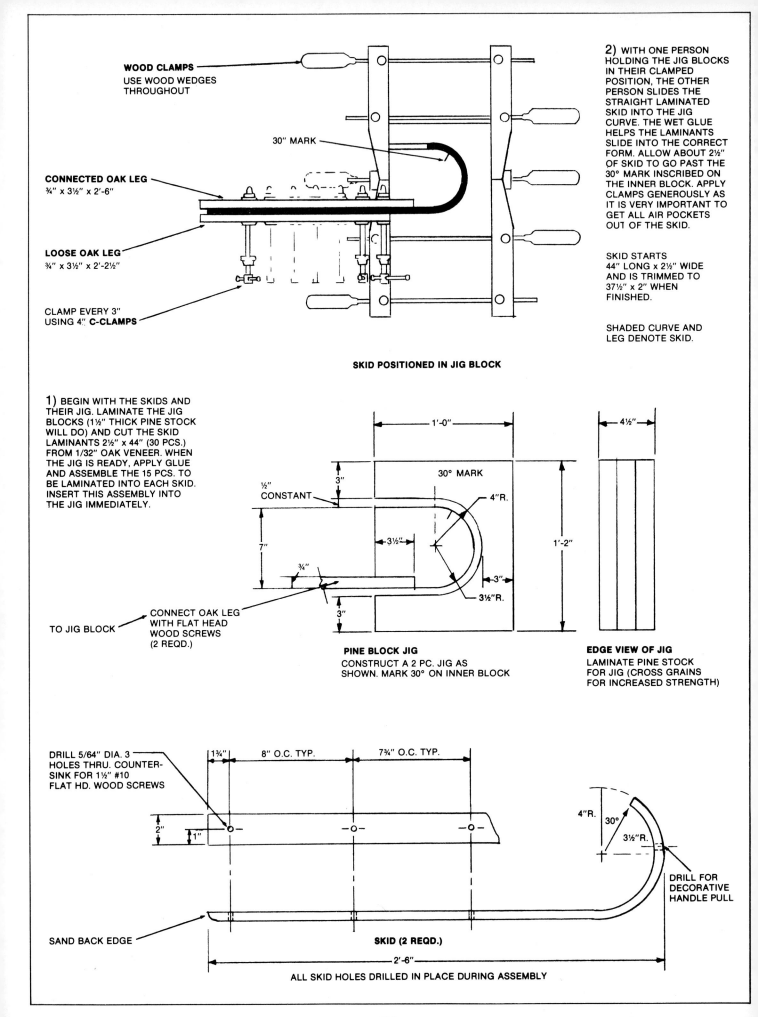

WOOD CLAMPS
USE WOOD WEDGES
THROUGHOUT

30" MARK

CONNECTED OAK LEG
¾" x 3½" x 2'-6"

LOOSE OAK LEG
¾" x 3½" x 2'-2½"

CLAMP EVERY 3"
USING 4" **C-CLAMPS**

2) WITH ONE PERSON
HOLDING THE JIG BLOCKS
IN THEIR CLAMPED
POSITION, THE OTHER
PERSON SLIDES THE
STRAIGHT LAMINATED
SKID INTO THE JIG
CURVE. THE WET GLUE
HELPS THE LAMINANTS
SLIDE INTO THE CORRECT
FORM. ALLOW ABOUT 2½"
OF SKID TO GO PAST THE
30° MARK INSCRIBED ON
THE INNER BLOCK. APPLY
CLAMPS GENEROUSLY AS
IT IS VERY IMPORTANT TO
GET ALL AIR POCKETS
OUT OF THE SKID.

SKID STARTS
44" LONG x 2½" WIDE
AND IS TRIMMED TO
37½" x 2" WHEN
FINISHED.

SHADED CURVE AND
LEG DENOTE SKID.

SKID POSITIONED IN JIG BLOCK

1) BEGIN WITH THE SKIDS AND
THEIR JIG. LAMINATE THE JIG
BLOCKS (1½" THICK PINE STOCK
WILL DO) AND CUT THE SKID
LAMINANTS 2½" x 44" (30 PCS.)
FROM 1/32" OAK VENEER. WHEN
THE JIG IS READY, APPLY GLUE
AND ASSEMBLE THE 15 PCS. TO
BE LAMINATED INTO EACH SKID.
INSERT THIS ASSEMBLY INTO
THE JIG IMMEDIATELY.

1'-0"

3"

½"
CONSTANT

30° MARK

4"R.

7"

3½"

1'-2"

¾"

3"

CONNECT OAK LEG
WITH FLAT HEAD
WOOD SCREWS
(2 REQD.)

TO JIG BLOCK

3"

3½"R.

PINE BLOCK JIG
CONSTRUCT A 2 PC. JIG AS
SHOWN. MARK 30° ON INNER BLOCK

4½"

EDGE VIEW OF JIG
LAMINATE PINE STOCK
FOR JIG (CROSS GRAINS
FOR INCREASED STRENGTH)

DRILL 5/64" DIA. 3
HOLES THRU. COUNTER-
SINK FOR 1½" #10
FLAT HD. WOOD SCREWS

1¾"

8" O.C. TYP.

7¾" O.C. TYP.

4"R.

30°

3½"R.

2"

1"

DRILL FOR
DECORATIVE
HANDLE PULL

SAND BACK EDGE

SKID (2 REQD.)

2'-6"

ALL SKID HOLES DRILLED IN PLACE DURING ASSEMBLY

74

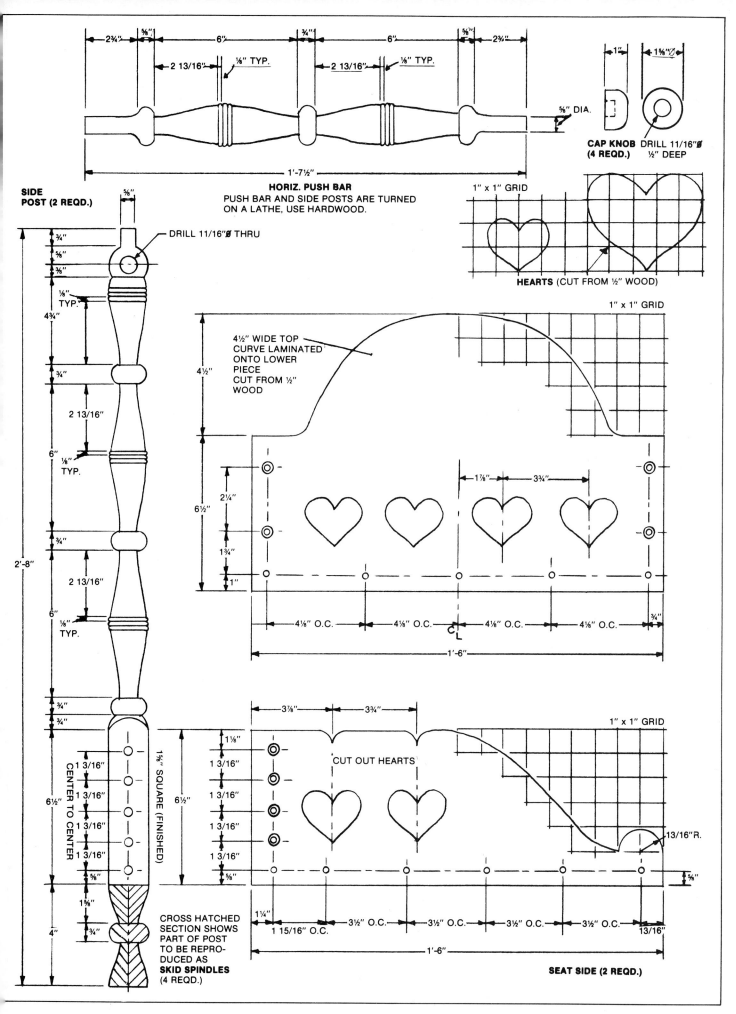

SIDE POST (2 REQD.)

⅝"

¾"
⅝"
⅜"

⅛" TYP.

4¾"

¾"

2 13/16"

6"

⅛" TYP.

¾"

2 13/16"

6"

⅛" TYP.

¾"

2'-8"

¾"

DRILL 11/16"∅ THRU

6½" CENTER TO CENTER

1 3/16"
1 3/16"
1 3/16"
1 3/16"

⅝"

1⅝"

¾"

4"

1⅝" SQUARE (FINISHED)

CROSS HATCHED SECTION SHOWS PART OF POST TO BE REPRODUCED AS **SKID SPINDLES** (4 REQD.)

HORIZ. PUSH BAR
PUSH BAR AND SIDE POSTS ARE TURNED ON A LATHE, USE HARDWOOD.

2¾" ⅝" 6" ¾" 6" ⅝" 2¾"

2 13/16" ⅛" TYP. 2 13/16" ⅛" TYP.

⅝" DIA.

1'-7½"

1" 1⅝"∅

CAP KNOB DRILL 11/16"∅
(4 REQD.) ½" DEEP

1" x 1" GRID

HEARTS (CUT FROM ½" WOOD)

1" x 1" GRID

4½" WIDE TOP CURVE LAMINATED ONTO LOWER PIECE CUT FROM ½" WOOD

4½"

6½"

2¼"

1¾"

1"

1⅞" 3¾"

4⅛" O.C. 4⅛" O.C. C L 4⅛" O.C. 4⅛" O.C. ¾"

1'-6"

3⅞" 3¾"

1⅛"

1 3/16"
1 3/16"
1 3/16"
1 3/16"

⅝"

CUT OUT HEARTS

6½"

13/16" R.

⅝"

1¼"

1 15/16" O.C. 3½" O.C. 3½" O.C. 3½" O.C. 3½" O.C. 13/16"

1'-6"

SEAT SIDE (2 REQD.)

75

5-Car Riding Train

What great fun for your children and their friends. No fighting over this toy—they can all take a ride. All cars disconnect and have a special wagon-type handle that attaches, so individual cars can be pulled, towed or pushed separately. Work people and passengers can be put into the coach and caboose seats and taken out again. Should last a lifetime.

Dimensions for each car given on following page.

Engine and Coal Car

When we say "ALL ABOARD", we mean climb aboard, for old 99 is ready to go. Engine cab has all the colored knobs and levers that the 2 engineers will need to help you keep this train on track. Set of four small front wheels turn for steering. Coal car wheels do not swivel, but car pivots on engine for turning. Engine, like other cars, has a handle that may be connected to it if you want to pull it. Handle also steers engine. Lots of fun.

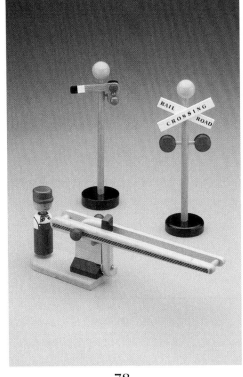

Track Accessories

When the gate is down and the red lights are on, everyone will know the train is coming. A valuable safety device for your little brother. The track signal, of course, tells you when there is a clear track ahead for the cannonball run.

Gondola Car

Another "tough job" car for your hauling needs. Will carry coal, barrels, or tall things that won't fit into the box car.

Box Car

No train is complete without a Box Car, and this one has sliding doors to open and close. Nice and sturdy for years of use.

Royal Coach

Has window seats for everyone, and 2 first class conductors to serve your every need. Top is hinged for easy access. Certainly First Class travel to wherever you want to go.

Kickapoo Valley Caboose

Has front and rear platform pegs to hold two trainmen. Top is hinged for inside access. Interior has a seat by middle window on each side for crewmen, and plenty of room for other "stuff".

Engine

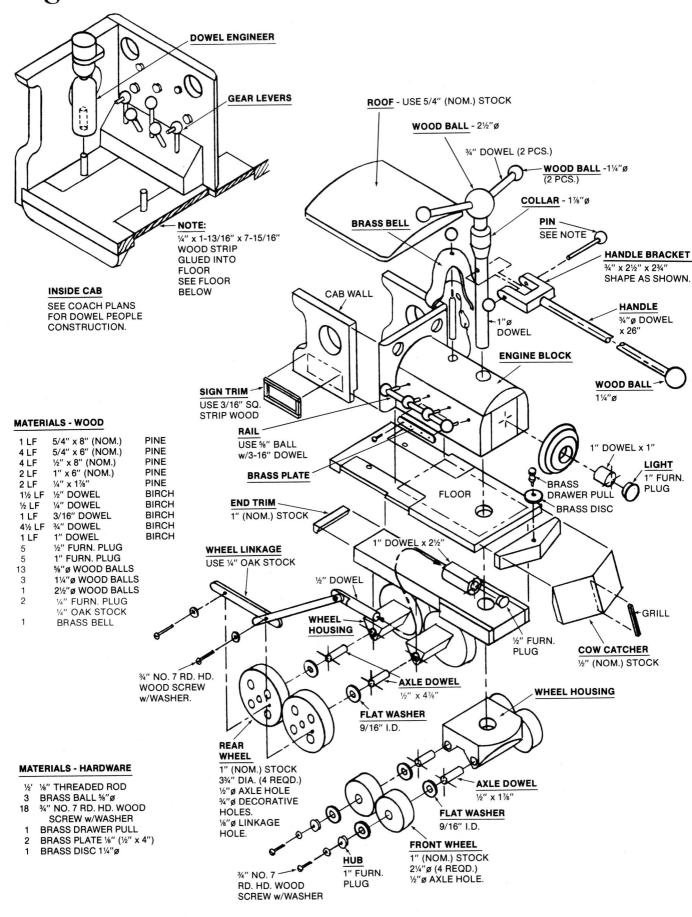

DOWEL ENGINEER

GEAR LEVERS

NOTE:
¼" x 1-13/16" x 7-15/16"
WOOD STRIP
GLUED INTO
FLOOR
SEE FLOOR
BELOW

INSIDE CAB

SEE COACH PLANS
FOR DOWEL PEOPLE
CONSTRUCTION.

ROOF - USE 5/4" (NOM.) STOCK

WOOD BALL - 2½"ø

¾" DOWEL (2 PCS.)

WOOD BALL -1¼"ø
(2 PCS.)

COLLAR - 1⅞"ø

BRASS BELL

PIN
SEE NOTE

HANDLE BRACKET
¾" x 2½" x 2¾"
SHAPE AS SHOWN.

CAB WALL

1"ø
DOWEL

ENGINE BLOCK

HANDLE
¾"ø DOWEL
x 26"

WOOD BALL
1¼"ø

SIGN TRIM
USE 3/16" SQ.
STRIP WOOD

RAIL
USE ⅝" BALL
w/3-16" DOWEL

BRASS PLATE

FLOOR

1" DOWEL x 1"

LIGHT
1" FURN.
PLUG

**BRASS
DRAWER PULL**

BRASS DISC

END TRIM
1" (NOM.) STOCK

1" DOWEL x 2½"

½" FURN.
PLUG

GRILL

COW CATCHER
½" (NOM.) STOCK

MATERIALS - WOOD

1 LF	5/4" x 8" (NOM.)	PINE
4 LF	5/4" x 6" (NOM.)	PINE
4 LF	½" x 8" (NOM.)	PINE
2 LF	1" x 6" (NOM.)	PINE
2 LF	¼" x 1⅞"	PINE
1½ LF	½" DOWEL	BIRCH
½ LF	¼" DOWEL	BIRCH
1 LF	3/16" DOWEL	BIRCH
4½ LF	¾" DOWEL	BIRCH
1 LF	1" DOWEL	BIRCH
5	½" FURN. PLUG	
5	1" FURN. PLUG	
13	⅝"ø WOOD BALLS	
3	1¼"ø WOOD BALLS	
1	2½"ø WOOD BALLS	
2	¼" FURN. PLUG	
	¼" OAK STOCK	
1	BRASS BELL	

WHEEL LINKAGE
USE ¼" OAK STOCK

½" DOWEL

**WHEEL
HOUSING**

¾" NO. 7 RD. HD.
WOOD SCREW
w/WASHER.

AXLE DOWEL
½" x 4⅞"

FLAT WASHER
9/16" I.D.

WHEEL HOUSING

**REAR
WHEEL**
1" (NOM.) STOCK
3¾" DIA. (4 REQD.)
½"ø AXLE HOLE
¾"ø DECORATIVE
HOLES.
⅛"ø LINKAGE
HOLE.

AXLE DOWEL
½" x 1⅞"

FLAT WASHER
9/16" I.D.

FRONT WHEEL
1" (NOM.) STOCK
2¼"ø (4 REQD.)
½"ø AXLE HOLE.

HUB
1" FURN.
PLUG

¾" NO. 7
RD. HD. WOOD
SCREW w/WASHER

MATERIALS - HARDWARE

½'	⅛" THREADED ROD
3	BRASS BALL ⅝"ø
18	¾" NO. 7 RD. HD. WOOD SCREW w/WASHER
1	BRASS DRAWER PULL
2	BRASS PLATE ⅛" (½" x 4")
1	BRASS DISC 1¼"ø

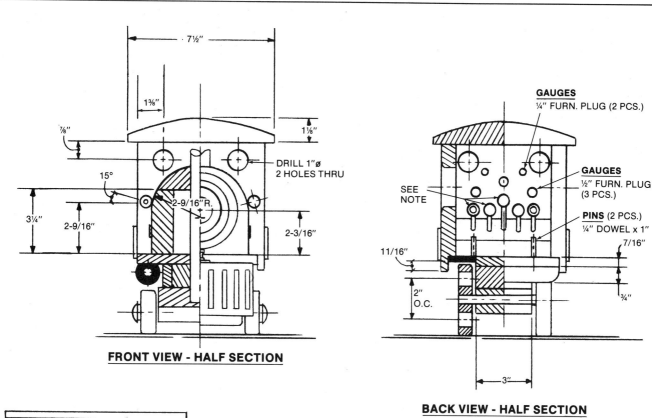

FRONT VIEW - HALF SECTION

DRILL 1"ø 2 HOLES THRU

2-9/16"R.

GAUGES
¼" FURN. PLUG (2 PCS.)

GAUGES
½" FURN. PLUG (3 PCS.)

PINS (2 PCS.)
¼" DOWEL x 1

SEE NOTE

BACK VIEW - HALF SECTION
NOTE: FOR GEAR LEVERS, USE ¼" DOWELS FITTED ON ⅝" DIA. WOOD BALLS. CUT TO FIT DURING CONSTRUCTION.

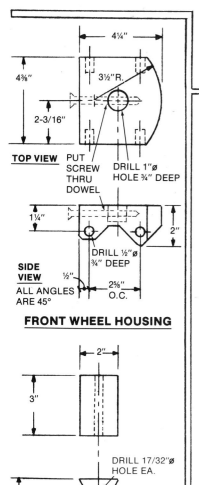

TOP VIEW

PUT SCREW THRU DOWEL

DRILL 1"ø HOLE ¾" DEEP

DRILL ½"ø ¾" DEEP

SIDE VIEW
ALL ANGLES ARE 45°

FRONT WHEEL HOUSING

DRILL 17/32"ø HOLE EA.

REAR WHEEL HOUSING

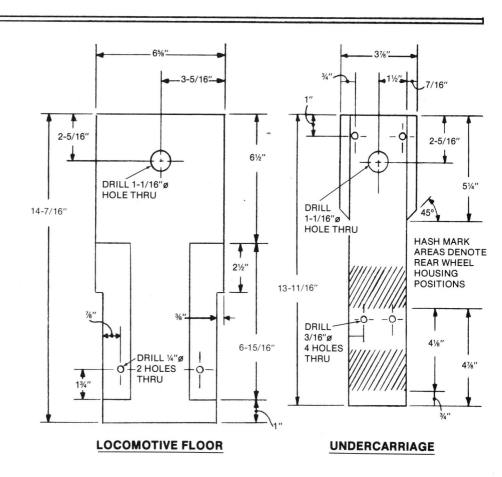

DRILL 1-1/16"ø HOLE THRU

DRILL ¼"ø 2 HOLES THRU

LOCOMOTIVE FLOOR

DRILL 1-1/16"ø HOLE THRU

HASH MARK AREAS DENOTE REAR WHEEL HOUSING POSITIONS

DRILL 3/16"ø 4 HOLES THRU

UNDERCARRIAGE

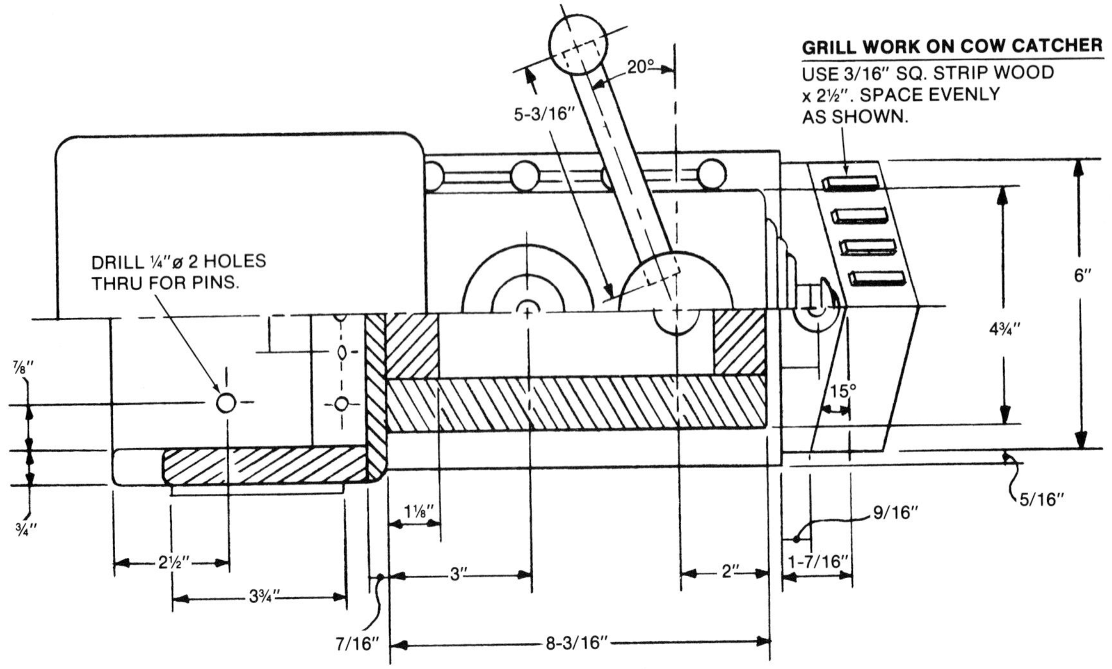
GRILL WORK ON COW CATCHER
USE 3/16" SQ. STRIP WOOD x 2½". SPACE EVENLY AS SHOWN.
DRILL ¼"ø 2 HOLES THRU FOR PINS.
5-3/16"
20°
6"
4¾"
15°
⅞"
¾"
5/16"
9/16"
1⅛"
1-7/16"
2½"
3"
2"
3¾"
7/16"
8-3/16"

TOP VIEW - HALF SECTION - LOCOMOTIVE

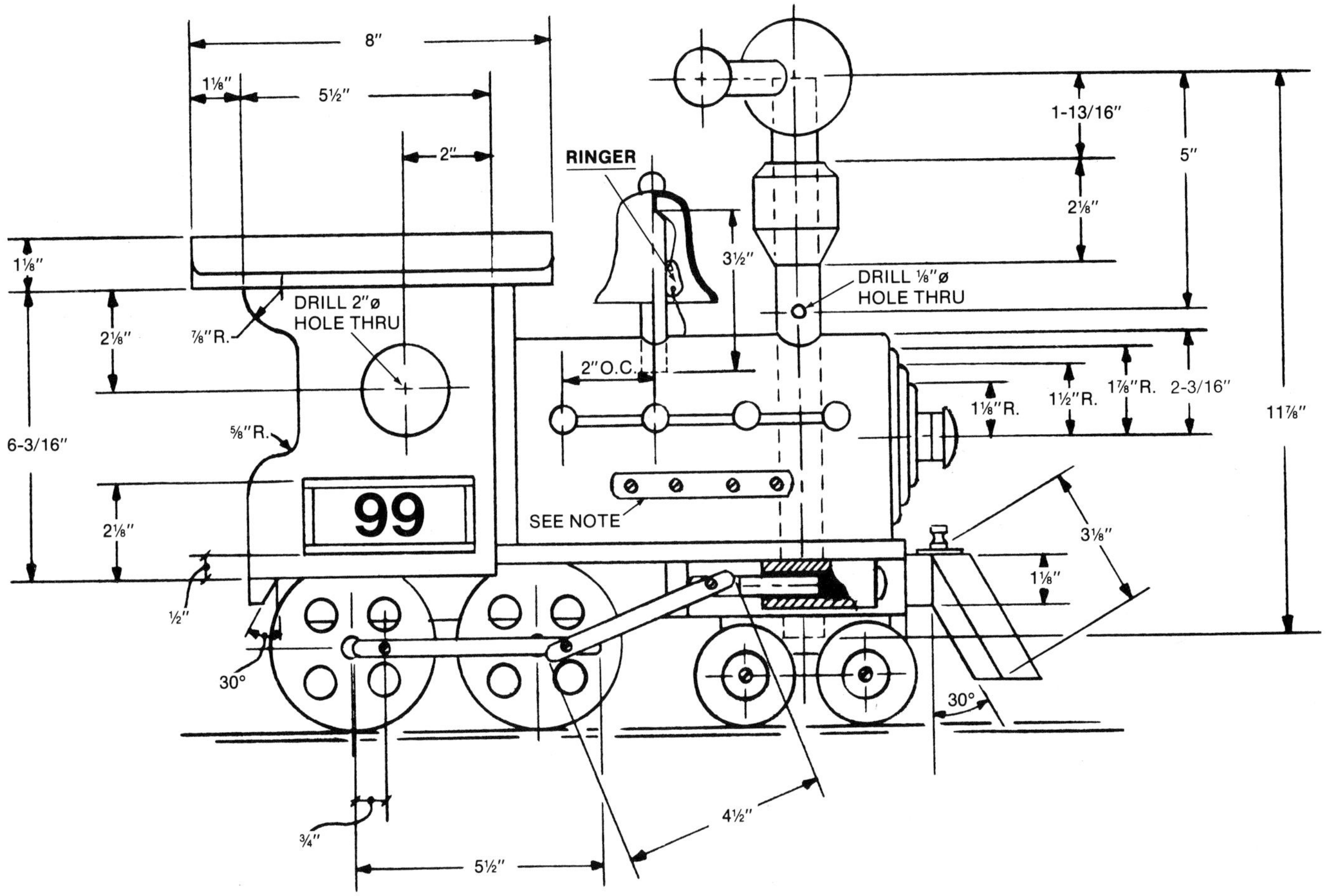
8"
1⅛"
5½"
2"
RINGER
1-13/16"
5"
2⅛"
3½"
DRILL ⅛"ø HOLE THRU
1⅛"
2⅛"
⅞"R.
DRILL 2"ø HOLE THRU
2"O.C.
1⅛"R.
1½"R.
1⅞"R.
2-3/16"
11⅞"
6-3/16"
⅝"R.
99
SEE NOTE
2⅛"
3⅛"
1⅛"
½"
30°
30°
4½"
¾"
5½"

SIDE VIEW - LOCOMOTIVE

USE 1" RUB-ON NUMBERS.
NOTE: AFFIX ⅛" x ½" x 4" BRASS PLATE TO SIDES. EVENLY SPACE ¾" NO. 7 RD. HD. WOOD SCREWS AS SHOWN.

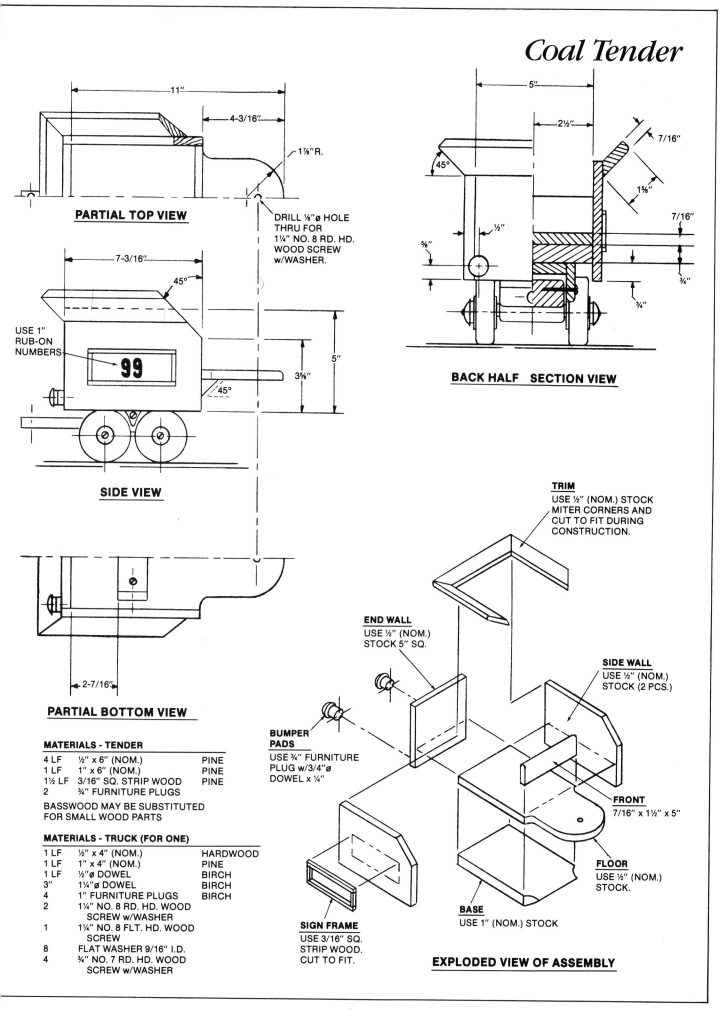

Coal Tender

PARTIAL TOP VIEW

11"

4-3/16"

1⅛"R.

DRILL ⅛"ø HOLE THRU FOR 1¼" NO. 8 RD. HD. WOOD SCREW w/WASHER.

SIDE VIEW

7-3/16"

45°

USE 1" RUB-ON NUMBERS

99

45°

3⅝"

5"

PARTIAL BOTTOM VIEW

2-7/16"

BACK HALF SECTION VIEW

5"

2½"

7/16"

1⅝"

7/16"

45°

½"

⅝"

¾"

¾"

MATERIALS - TENDER

4 LF	½" x 6" (NOM.)	PINE
1 LF	1" x 6" (NOM.)	PINE
1½ LF	3/16" SQ. STRIP WOOD	PINE
2	¾" FURNITURE PLUGS	

BASSWOOD MAY BE SUBSTITUTED FOR SMALL WOOD PARTS

MATERIALS - TRUCK (FOR ONE)

1 LF	½" x 4" (NOM.)	HARDWOOD
1 LF	1" x 4" (NOM.)	PINE
1 LF	½"ø DOWEL	BIRCH
3"	1¼"ø DOWEL	BIRCH
4	1" FURNITURE PLUGS	BIRCH
2	1¼" NO. 8 RD. HD. WOOD SCREW w/WASHER	
1	1¼" NO. 8 FLT. HD. WOOD SCREW	
8	FLAT WASHER 9/16" I.D.	
4	¾" NO. 7 RD. HD. WOOD SCREW w/WASHER	

TRIM
USE ½" (NOM.) STOCK MITER CORNERS AND CUT TO FIT DURING CONSTRUCTION.

END WALL
USE ½" (NOM.) STOCK 5" SQ.

SIDE WALL
USE ½" (NOM.) STOCK (2 PCS.)

BUMPER PADS
USE ¾" FURNITURE PLUG w/3/4"ø DOWEL x ¼"

FRONT
7/16" x 1½" x 5"

FLOOR
USE ½" (NOM.) STOCK.

BASE
USE 1" (NOM.) STOCK

SIGN FRAME
USE 3/16" SQ. STRIP WOOD. CUT TO FIT.

EXPLODED VIEW OF ASSEMBLY

Coach

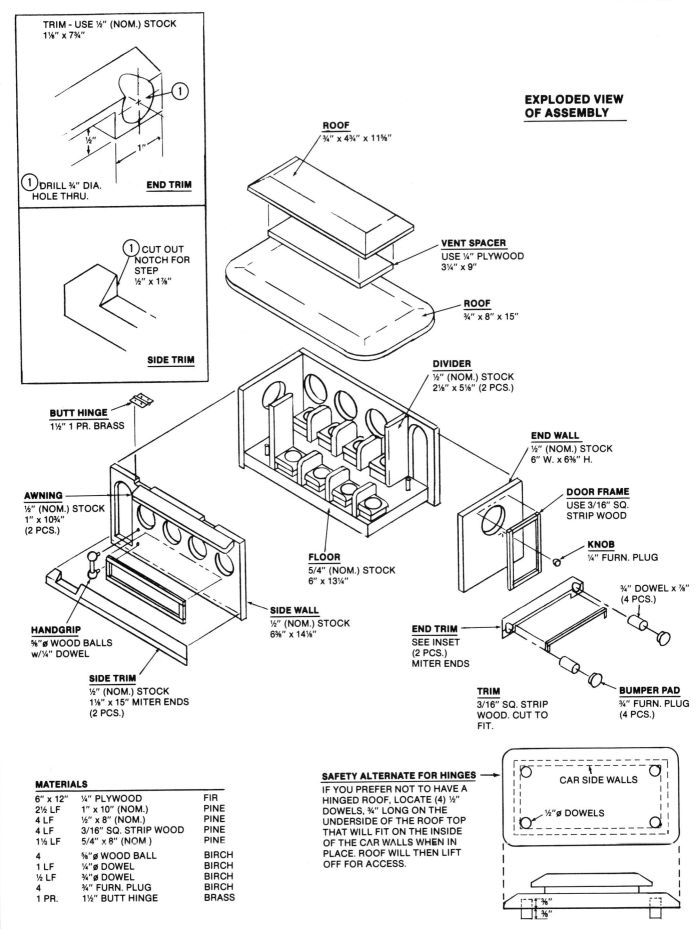

EXPLODED VIEW OF ASSEMBLY

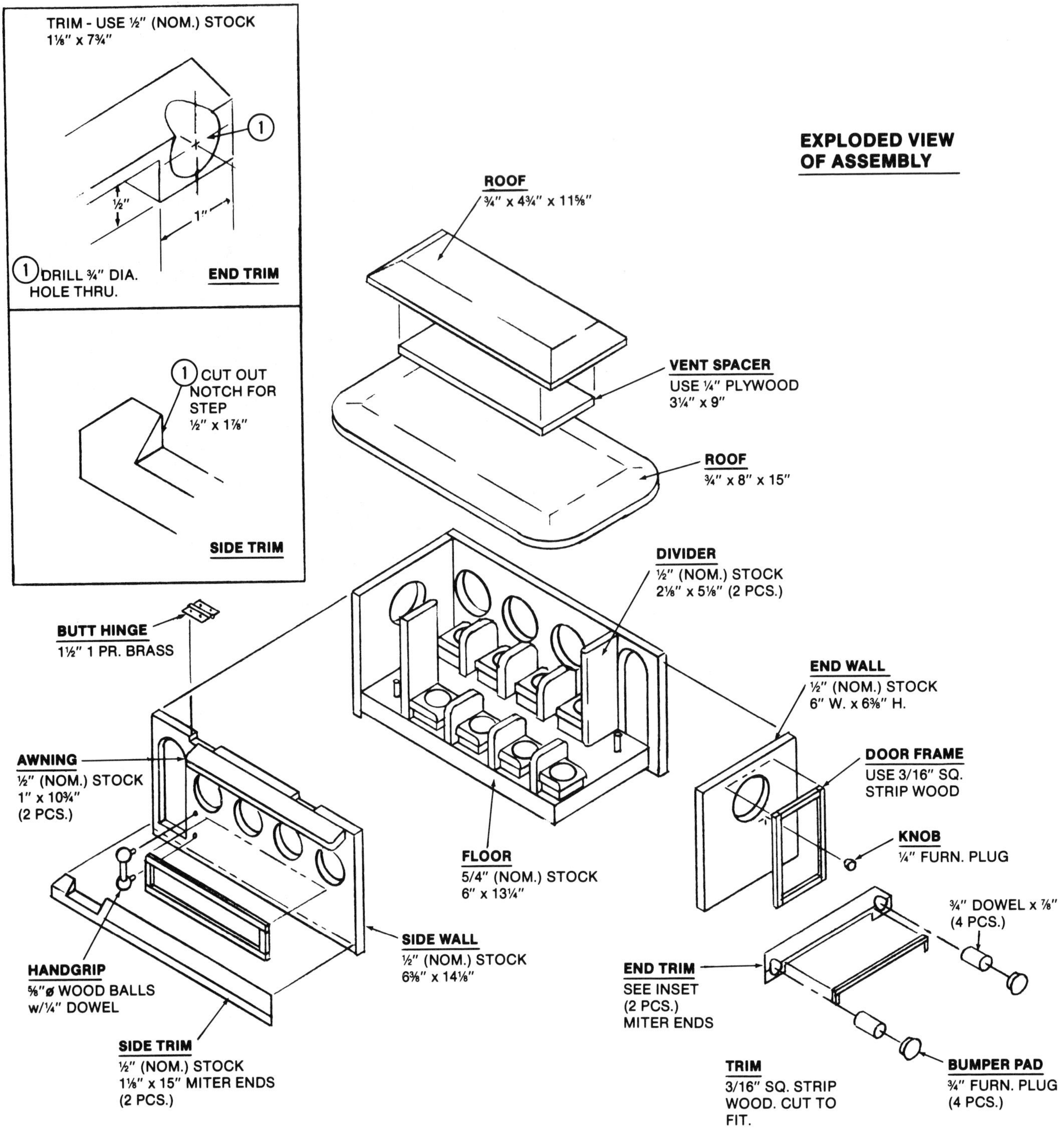
TRIM - USE ½" (NOM.) STOCK
1⅛" x 7¾"
½"
1"
① DRILL ¾" DIA. HOLE THRU.
END TRIM
① CUT OUT NOTCH FOR STEP
½" x 1⅞"
SIDE TRIM
ROOF
¾" x 4¾" x 11⅝"
VENT SPACER
USE ¼" PLYWOOD
3¼" x 9"
ROOF
¾" x 8" x 15"
DIVIDER
½" (NOM.) STOCK
2⅛" x 5⅛" (2 PCS.)
BUTT HINGE
1½" 1 PR. BRASS
END WALL
½" (NOM.) STOCK
6" W. x 6⅜" H.
AWNING
½" (NOM.) STOCK
1" x 10¾"
(2 PCS.)
DOOR FRAME
USE 3/16" SQ. STRIP WOOD
KNOB
¼" FURN. PLUG
FLOOR
5/4" (NOM.) STOCK
6" x 13¼"
¾" DOWEL x ⅞"
(4 PCS.)
SIDE WALL
½" (NOM.) STOCK
6⅜" x 14⅛"
HANDGRIP
⅝"ø WOOD BALLS
w/¼" DOWEL
END TRIM
SEE INSET
(2 PCS.)
MITER ENDS
SIDE TRIM
½" (NOM.) STOCK
1⅛" x 15" MITER ENDS
(2 PCS.)
TRIM
3/16" SQ. STRIP WOOD. CUT TO FIT.
BUMPER PAD
¾" FURN. PLUG
(4 PCS.)

SAFETY ALTERNATE FOR HINGES

IF YOU PREFER NOT TO HAVE A HINGED ROOF, LOCATE (4) ½" DOWELS, ¾" LONG ON THE UNDERSIDE OF THE ROOF TOP THAT WILL FIT ON THE INSIDE OF THE CAR WALLS WHEN IN PLACE. ROOF WILL THEN LIFT OFF FOR ACCESS.

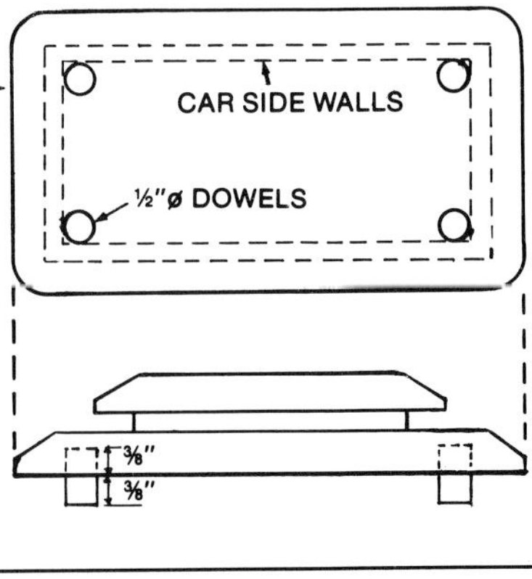
CAR SIDE WALLS
½"ø DOWELS
⅜"
⅜"

MATERIALS

6" x 12"	¼" PLYWOOD	FIR
2½ LF	1" x 10" (NOM.)	PINE
4 LF	½" x 8" (NOM.)	PINE
4 LF	3/16" SQ. STRIP WOOD	PINE
1½ LF	5/4" x 8" (NOM.)	PINE
4	⅝"ø WOOD BALL	BIRCH
1 LF	¼"ø DOWEL	BIRCH
½ LF	¾"ø DOWEL	BIRCH
4	¾" FURN. PLUG	BIRCH
1 PR.	1½" BUTT HINGE	BRASS

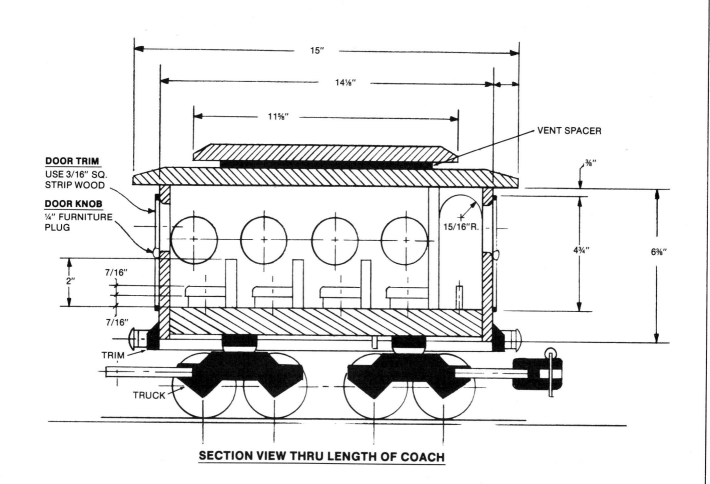

15"

14⅛"

11⅝"

VENT SPACER

DOOR TRIM
USE 3/16" SQ.
STRIP WOOD

DOOR KNOB
¼" FURNITURE
PLUG

⅜"

15/16"R.

4¾"

6⅜"

2"

7/16"

7/16"

TRIM

TRUCK

SECTION VIEW THRU LENGTH OF COACH

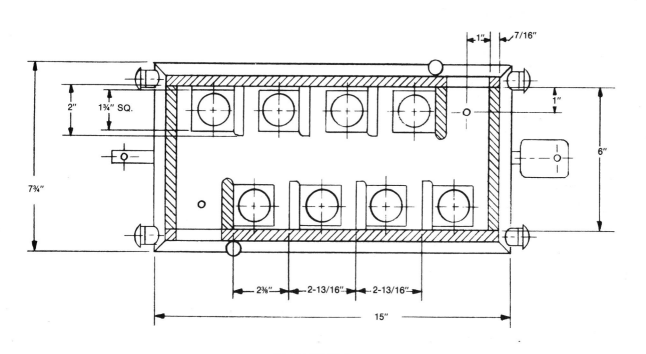

1"

7/16"

2"

1¾" SQ.

1"

6"

7¾"

2⅜"

2-13/16"

2-13/16"

15"

PLAN VIEW OF COACH

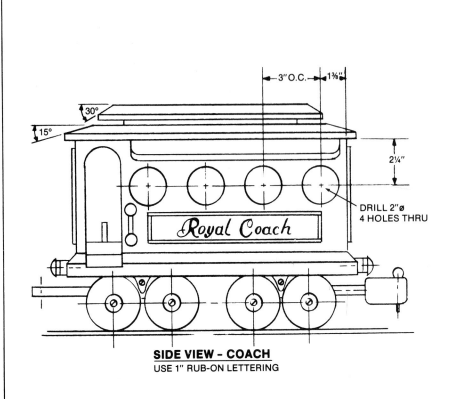

30°

15°

3" O.C.   1⅜"

2¼"

DRILL 2"ø
4 HOLES THRU

Royal Coach

SIDE VIEW – COACH
USE 1" RUB-ON LETTERING

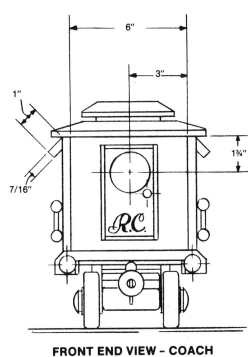

6"

3"

1"

7/16"

1¾"

R.C.

FRONT END VIEW – COACH

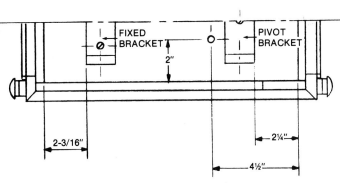

FIXED
BRACKET

PIVOT
BRACKET

2"

2-3/16"   2¼"

4½"

PARTIAL BOTTOM VIEW

DASHED LINES SHOW
HOW ROOF OF
COACH OPENS
TO ALLOW
INSIDE ACCESS.

DRILL 2"ø
HOLE THRU
EA. END.

45°

**SECTION VIEW THRU
WIDTH OF COACH**
BLACK AREAS DENOTE
TRUCK BRACKET, SIDE TRIM,
AND ROOF VENT SPACER

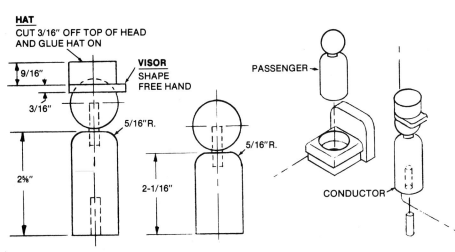

HAT
CUT 3/16" OFF TOP OF HEAD
AND GLUE HAT ON

9/16"

3/16"

VISOR
SHAPE
FREE HAND

5/16"R.

2⅝"

PASSENGER

5/16"R.

2-1/16"

PASSENGER

CONDUCTOR

**CONDUCTOR,
ENGINEER**
1¼"ø WOOD BALL
1¼"ø DOWEL
¼"ø DOWEL x 1" (NECK)

PASSENGER
1¼"ø WOOD BALL
1¼"ø DOWEL

Undercarriage

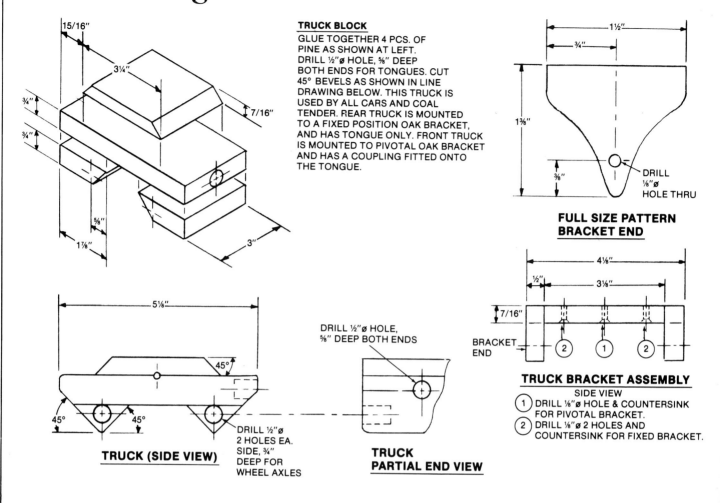

TRUCK BLOCK
GLUE TOGETHER 4 PCS. OF PINE AS SHOWN AT LEFT. DRILL ½"ø HOLE, ⅝" DEEP BOTH ENDS FOR TONGUES. CUT 45° BEVELS AS SHOWN IN LINE DRAWING BELOW. THIS TRUCK IS USED BY ALL CARS AND COAL TENDER. REAR TRUCK IS MOUNTED TO A FIXED POSITION OAK BRACKET, AND HAS TONGUE ONLY. FRONT TRUCK IS MOUNTED TO A PIVOTAL OAK BRACKET AND HAS A COUPLING FITTED ONTO THE TONGUE.

FULL SIZE PATTERN BRACKET END

DRILL ⅛"ø HOLE THRU

DRILL ½"ø HOLE, ⅝" DEEP BOTH ENDS

TRUCK (SIDE VIEW)

DRILL ½"ø 2 HOLES EA. SIDE, ¾" DEEP FOR WHEEL AXLES

TRUCK PARTIAL END VIEW

TRUCK BRACKET ASSEMBLY
SIDE VIEW
① DRILL ⅛"ø HOLE & COUNTERSINK FOR PIVOTAL BRACKET.
② DRILL ⅛"ø 2 HOLES AND COUNTERSINK FOR FIXED BRACKET.
BRACKET END

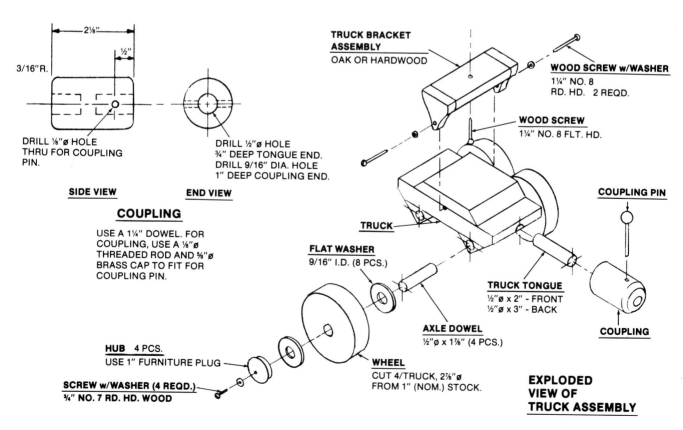

3/16"R.

DRILL ⅛"ø HOLE THRU FOR COUPLING PIN.

DRILL ½"ø HOLE ¾" DEEP TONGUE END. DRILL 9/16" DIA. HOLE 1" DEEP COUPLING END.

SIDE VIEW   **END VIEW**

COUPLING

USE A 1¼" DOWEL. FOR COUPLING, USE A ⅛"ø THREADED ROD AND ⅝"ø BRASS CAP TO FIT FOR COUPLING PIN.

HUB 4 PCS.
USE 1" FURNITURE PLUG

SCREW w/WASHER (4 REQD.)
¾" NO. 7 RD. HD. WOOD

FLAT WASHER
9/16" I.D. (8 PCS.)

WHEEL
CUT 4/TRUCK, 2⅞"ø
FROM 1" (NOM.) STOCK.

AXLE DOWEL
½"ø x 1⅞" (4 PCS.)

TRUCK TONGUE
½"ø x 2" - FRONT
½"ø x 3" - BACK

TRUCK BRACKET ASSEMBLY
OAK OR HARDWOOD

WOOD SCREW w/WASHER
1¼" NO. 8
RD. HD.   2 REQD.

WOOD SCREW
1¼" NO. 8 FLT. HD.

COUPLING PIN

TRUCK

COUPLING

EXPLODED VIEW OF TRUCK ASSEMBLY

Boxcar

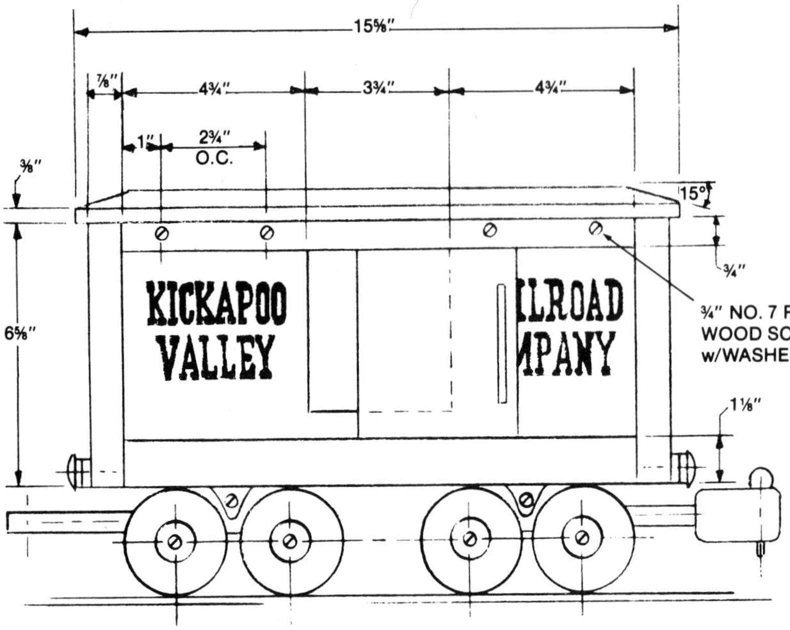
15⅝"
⅞"
4¾"
3¾"
4¾"
1"
2¾" O.C.
⅜"
15°
¾"
6⅝"
KICKAPOO VALLEY
ILROAD
MPANY
¾" NO. 7 RD. HD. WOOD SCREW w/WASHER (8 REQD.)
1⅛"

SIDE VIEW - BOX CAR

USE 1" RUB-ON LETTERING.
SLIDING DOOR - USE ½" (NOM.) STOCK 4⅛" W. x 5-3/16" H. RABBET ENDS ¼" x 3/16" DEEP. (2 REQD.)

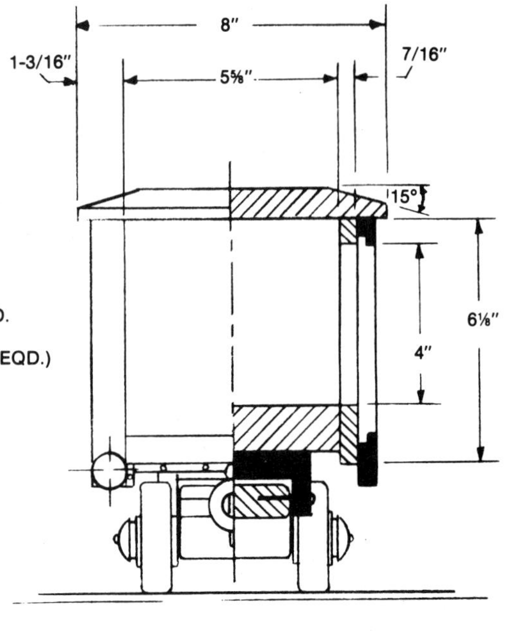
8"
1-3/16"
5⅝"
7/16"
15°
6⅛"
4"

END VIEW - BOX CAR

HALF SECTION

BLACK AREAS DENOTE SIDE TRIM & TRUCK BRACKET.

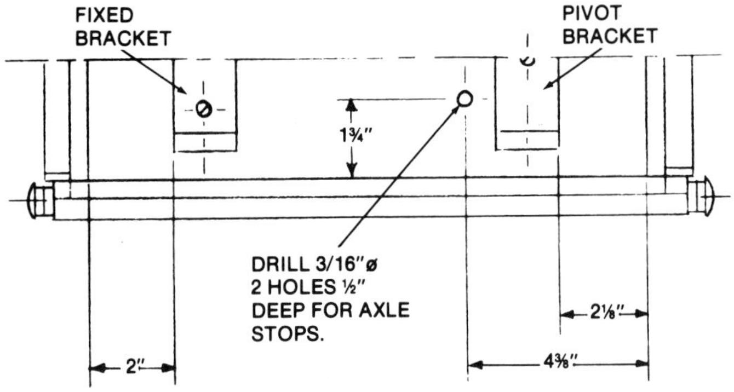
FIXED BRACKET
PIVOT BRACKET
1¾"
DRILL 3/16"ø 2 HOLES ½" DEEP FOR AXLE STOPS.
2⅛"
2"
4⅜"

PARTIAL BOTTOM VIEW

EXPLODED VIEW OF ASSEMBLY

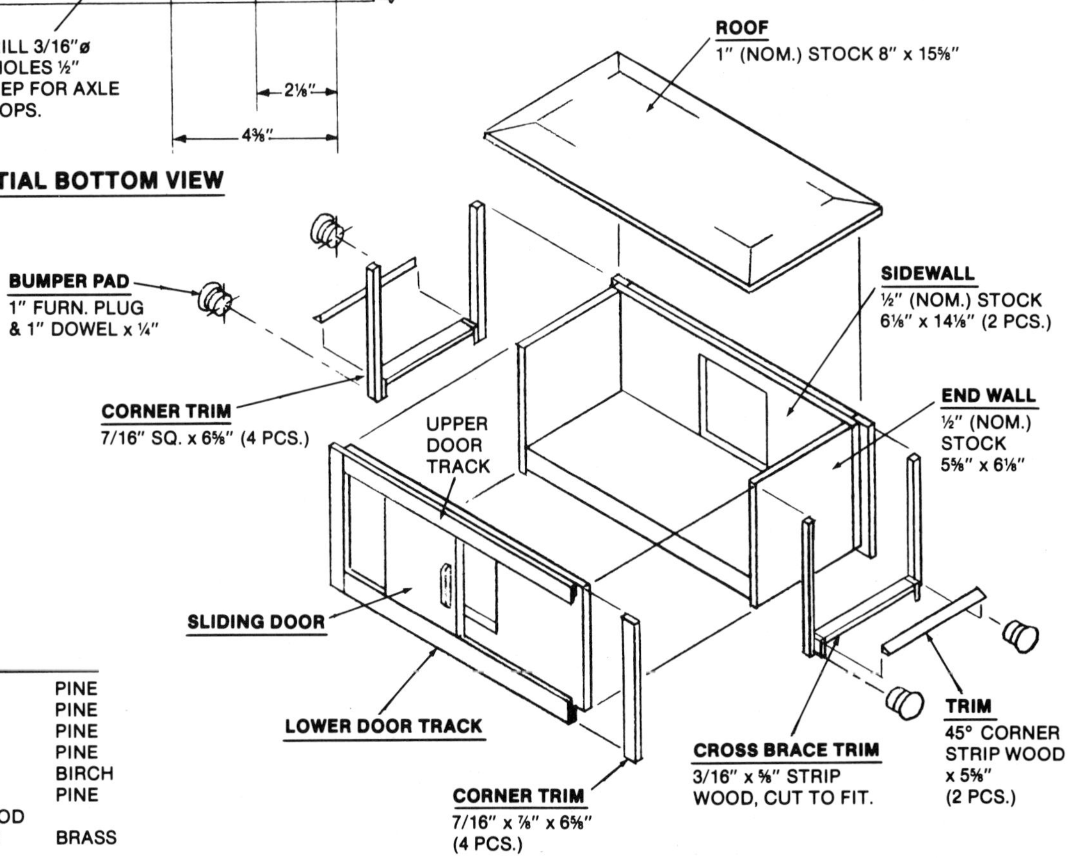
ROOF
1" (NOM.) STOCK 8" x 15⅝"
BUMPER PAD
1" FURN. PLUG & 1" DOWEL x ¼"
SIDEWALL
½" (NOM.) STOCK 6⅛" x 14⅛" (2 PCS.)
CORNER TRIM
7/16" SQ. x 6⅝" (4 PCS.)
UPPER DOOR TRACK
END WALL
½" (NOM.) STOCK 5⅝" x 6⅛"
SLIDING DOOR
LOWER DOOR TRACK
TRIM
45° CORNER STRIP WOOD x 5⅝" (2 PCS.)
CROSS BRACE TRIM
3/16" x ⅝" STRIP WOOD, CUT TO FIT.
CORNER TRIM
7/16" x ⅞" x 6⅝" (4 PCS.)

MATERIALS

5 LF	½" x 8" (NOM.)	PINE
1½ LF	1" x 10" (NOM.)	PINE
1½ LF	3/16" x ⅝" STRIP	PINE
4"	1"ø DOWEL	PINE
4	1" FURNITURE PLUG	BIRCH
1½ LF	5/4" x 8" (NOM.)	PINE
4	¾" NO. 7 RD. HD. WOOD SCREW w/WASHER	BRASS

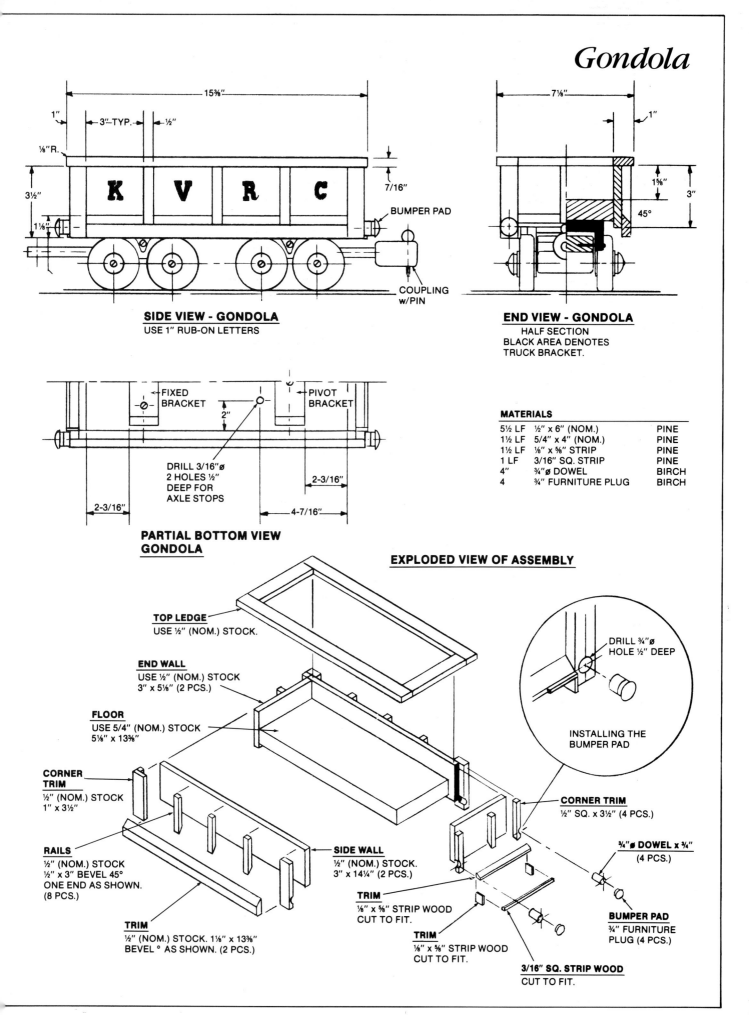

Gondola

SIDE VIEW - GONDOLA
USE 1" RUB-ON LETTERS

15⅜"
3"—TYP.
1"
½"
⅛"R.
3½"
1⅛"
7/16"
BUMPER PAD
COUPLING w/PIN

END VIEW - GONDOLA
HALF SECTION
BLACK AREA DENOTES
TRUCK BRACKET.

7⅛"
1"
1⅝"
3"
45°

PARTIAL BOTTOM VIEW GONDOLA
FIXED BRACKET
PIVOT BRACKET
2"
DRILL 3/16"ø
2 HOLES ½"
DEEP FOR
AXLE STOPS
2-3/16"
2-3/16"
4-7/16"

MATERIALS

5½ LF	½" x 6" (NOM.)	PINE
1½ LF	5/4" x 4" (NOM.)	PINE
1½ LF	⅛" x ⅝" STRIP	PINE
1 LF	3/16" SQ. STRIP	PINE
4"	¾"ø DOWEL	BIRCH
4	¾" FURNITURE PLUG	BIRCH

EXPLODED VIEW OF ASSEMBLY

TOP LEDGE
USE ½" (NOM.) STOCK.

END WALL
USE ½" (NOM.) STOCK
3" x 5⅛" (2 PCS.)

FLOOR
USE 5/4" (NOM.) STOCK
5⅛" x 13⅜"

CORNER TRIM
½" (NOM.) STOCK
1" x 3½"

RAILS
½" (NOM.) STOCK
½" x 3" BEVEL 45°
ONE END AS SHOWN.
(8 PCS.)

TRIM
½" (NOM.) STOCK. 1⅛" x 13⅜"
BEVEL ° AS SHOWN. (2 PCS.)

SIDE WALL
½" (NOM.) STOCK.
3" x 14¼" (2 PCS.)

TRIM
⅛" x ⅝" STRIP WOOD
CUT TO FIT.

TRIM
⅛" x ⅝" STRIP WOOD
CUT TO FIT.

3/16" SQ. STRIP WOOD
CUT TO FIT.

DRILL ¾"ø
HOLE ½" DEEP

INSTALLING THE
BUMPER PAD

CORNER TRIM
½" SQ. x 3½" (4 PCS.)

¾"ø DOWEL x ¾"
(4 PCS.)

BUMPER PAD
¾" FURNITURE
PLUG (4 PCS.)

Caboose

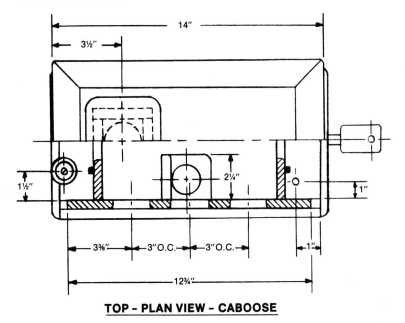

TOP – PLAN VIEW – CABOOSE

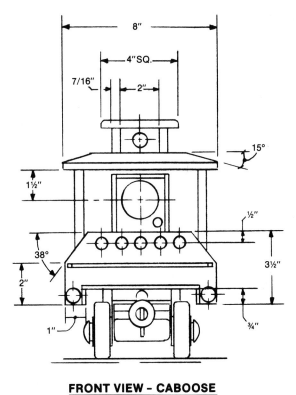

FRONT VIEW – CABOOSE

DRILL ¾" ø HOLE THRU EA. SIDE

DRILL 2" ø 3 HOLES THRU

1½" BUTT HINGE

1⅜"R.

HAND BRAKE

KICKAPOO VALLEY RAILROAD CO.

SIDE VIEW – CABOOSE
USE 1" RUB-ON LETTERING

DRILL ½" ø 5 HOLES THRU SPACE EVENLY.

CAB

BACK VIEW – HALF SECTION

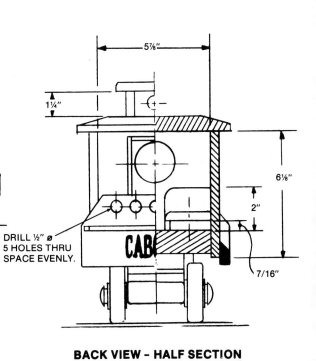

DRILL 3/16" ø 2 HOLES ¼" DEEP FOR AXLE STOPS

FIXED BRACKET

PIVOT BRACKET

PARTIAL BOTTOM VIEW

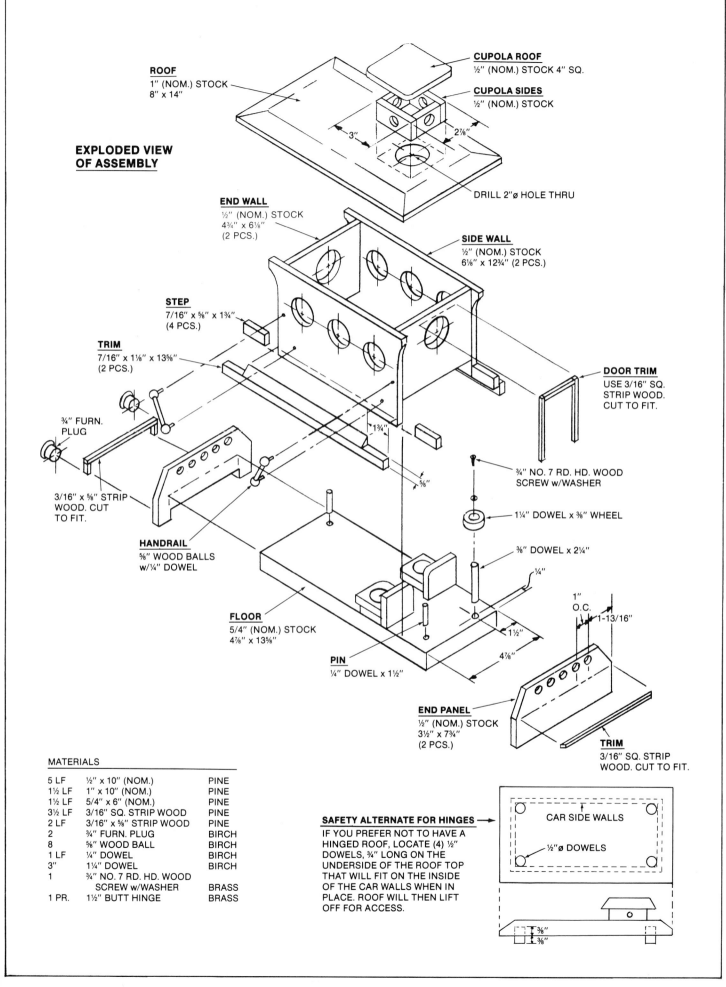

EXPLODED VIEW OF ASSEMBLY

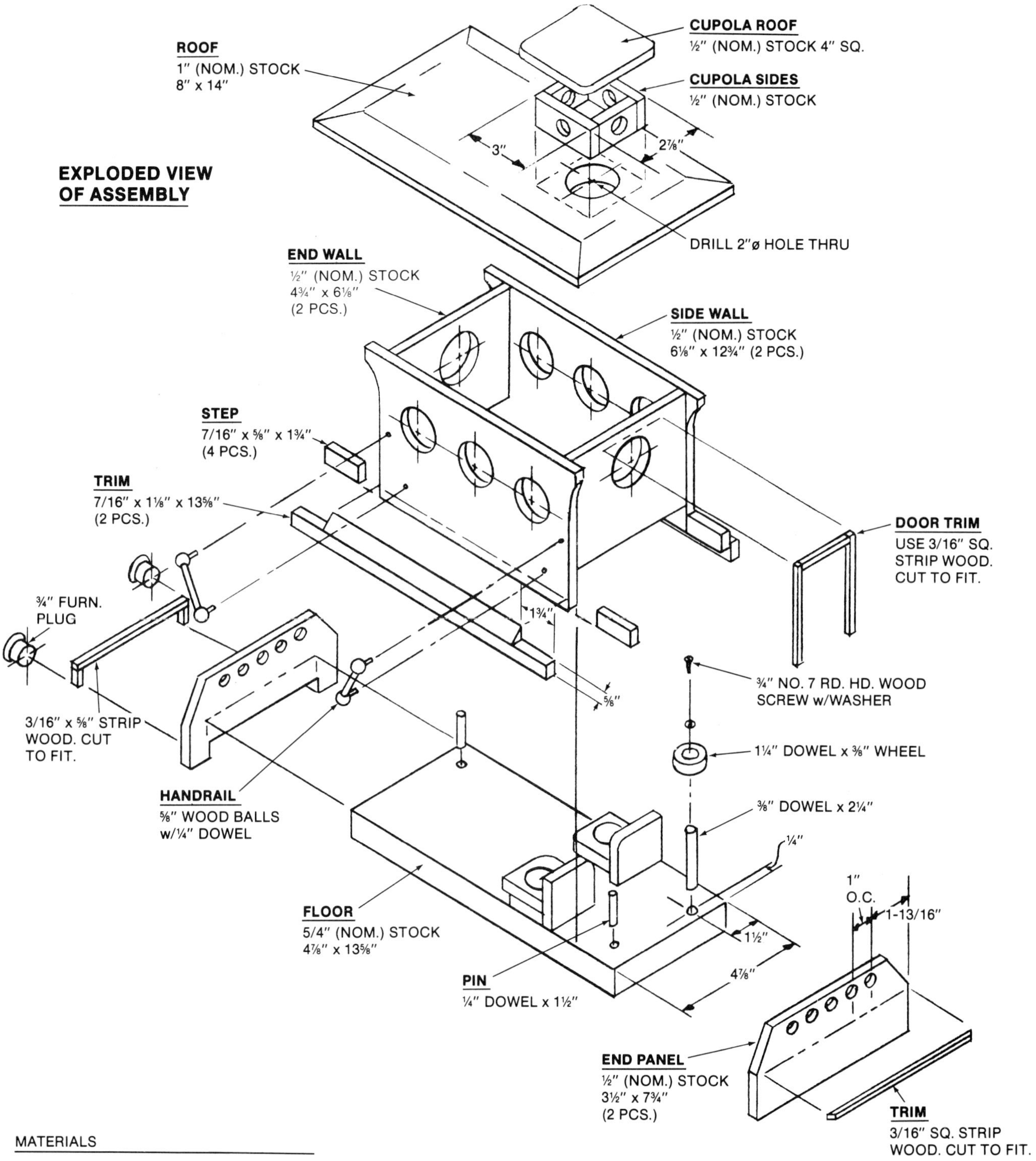
ROOF
1" (NOM.) STOCK
8" x 14"
CUPOLA ROOF
½" (NOM.) STOCK 4" SQ.
CUPOLA SIDES
½" (NOM.) STOCK
3"
2⅞"
DRILL 2"ø HOLE THRU
END WALL
½" (NOM.) STOCK
4¾" x 6⅛"
(2 PCS.)
SIDE WALL
½" (NOM.) STOCK
6⅛" x 12¾" (2 PCS.)
STEP
7/16" x ⅝" x 1¾"
(4 PCS.)
TRIM
7/16" x 1⅛" x 13⅝"
(2 PCS.)
DOOR TRIM
USE 3/16" SQ.
STRIP WOOD.
CUT TO FIT.
¾" FURN.
PLUG
1¾"
⅝"
¾" NO. 7 RD. HD. WOOD
SCREW w/WASHER
3/16" x ⅝" STRIP
WOOD. CUT
TO FIT.
1¼" DOWEL x ⅜" WHEEL
HANDRAIL
⅝" WOOD BALLS
w/¼" DOWEL
⅜" DOWEL x 2¼"
¼"
1"
O.C.
1-13/16"
FLOOR
5/4" (NOM.) STOCK
4⅞" x 13⅝"
1½"
4⅞"
PIN
¼" DOWEL x 1½"
END PANEL
½" (NOM.) STOCK
3½" x 7¾"
(2 PCS.)
TRIM
3/16" SQ. STRIP
WOOD. CUT TO FIT.

MATERIALS

5 LF	½" x 10" (NOM.)	PINE
1½ LF	1" x 10" (NOM.)	PINE
1½ LF	5/4" x 6" (NOM.)	PINE
3½ LF	3/16" SQ. STRIP WOOD	PINE
2 LF	3/16" x ⅝" STRIP WOOD	PINE
2	¾" FURN. PLUG	BIRCH
8	⅝" WOOD BALL	BIRCH
1 LF	¼" DOWEL	BIRCH
3"	1¼" DOWEL	BIRCH
1	¾" NO. 7 RD. HD. WOOD SCREW w/WASHER	BRASS
1 PR.	1½" BUTT HINGE	BRASS

SAFETY ALTERNATE FOR HINGES →

IF YOU PREFER NOT TO HAVE A HINGED ROOF, LOCATE (4) ½" DOWELS, ¾" LONG ON THE UNDERSIDE OF THE ROOF TOP THAT WILL FIT ON THE INSIDE OF THE CAR WALLS WHEN IN PLACE. ROOF WILL THEN LIFT OFF FOR ACCESS.

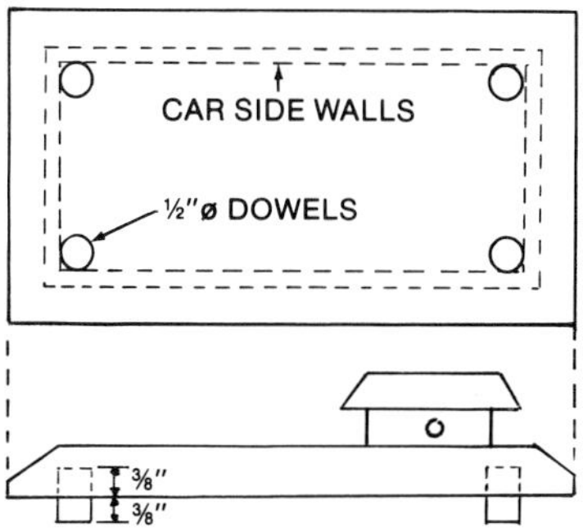
CAR SIDE WALLS
½"ø DOWELS
⅜"
⅜"

Bumpy Road Convoy

If you like a lot of ups and downs, then this is for you. A nice little action toy that allows little ones to pull their passengers anywhere. Offset axles move people up and down as the car is pulled along.

Bumpy Road Convoy

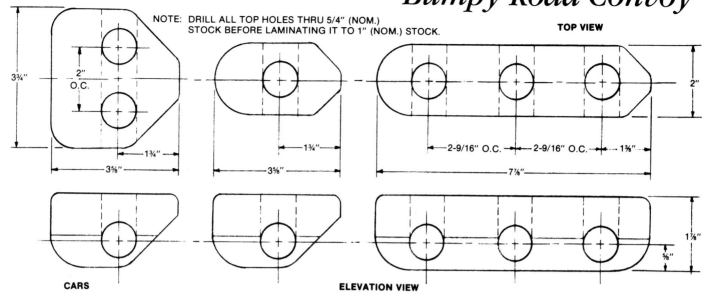

NOTE: DRILL ALL TOP HOLES THRU 5/4" (NOM.) STOCK BEFORE LAMINATING IT TO 1" (NOM.) STOCK.

CARS

ELEVATION VIEW

CARS ARE MADE FROM 5/4" (NOM.) STOCK, LAMINATED TO 1" (NOM.) STOCK AS SHOWN. ALL HOLES ARE 1" DIA. ALL ANGLES ARE 45° AND ALL ROUTED EDGES ARE 3/16" R.

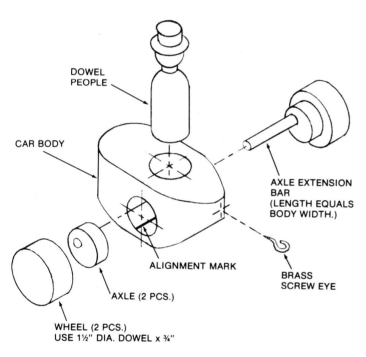

DOWEL PEOPLE

CAR BODY

AXLE EXTENSION BAR (LENGTH EQUALS BODY WIDTH.)

ALIGNMENT MARK

BRASS SCREW EYE

AXLE (2 PCS.)

WHEEL (2 PCS.) USE 1½" DIA. DOWEL x ¾"

EXPLODED VIEW OF CAR ASSEMBLY

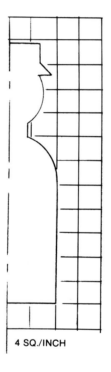

4 SQ./INCH

DOWEL PEOPLE
TURN ON LATHE USING 1" DIA. DOWEL. NOTE HAT VARIATIONS IN PICTORAL VIEW.

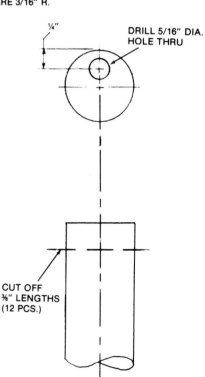

DRILL 5/16" DIA. HOLE THRU

CUT OFF ⅜" LENGTHS (12 PCS.)

WHEEL AXLE
USE 1" DIA. DOWEL. DRILL 5/16" DIA. HOLE AS DEEP AS POSSIBLE. CUT OFF AXLES AS SHOWN.

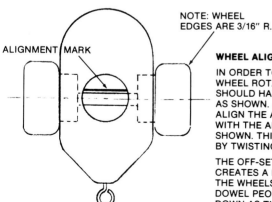

NOTE: WHEEL EDGES ARE 3/16" R.

ALIGNMENT MARK

WHEEL ALIGNMENT

IN ORDER TO ASSURE PROPER WHEEL ROTATION, ALL AXLE HOLES SHOULD HAVE AN ALIGNMENT MARK AS SHOWN. AFTER WHEEL ASSEMBLY, ALIGN THE AXLE EXTENSION BAR WITH THE ALIGNMENT MARK AS SHOWN. THIS CAN BE DONE EASILY BY TWISTING THE WHEELS.

THE OFF-SET AXLE EXTENSION BAR CREATES A PISTON-LIKE ACTION AS THE WHEELS ROTATE CAUSING THE DOWEL PEOPLE TO MOVE UP AND DOWN AS THE TOY IS PULLED ALONG.

MATERIALS:

2	L.F.	5/4" x 3" (NOM.)	PINE
2	L.F.	1" x 3" (NOM.)	PINE
1½	L.F.	5/16" DOWEL	BIRCH
2½	L.F.	1" DOWEL	BIRCH
1	L.F.	1½" DOWEL	BIRCH
7		½" SCREW EYE	BRASS
2	Ft.	NYLON STRETCH CORD	
1		1" WOOD BALL	BIRCH

Glue, Varnish and Quick Dry Enamel Paints as needed.

The Belly Full Dumper

Here is an old-fashioned, heavy-duty truck that has size, shape and color co-ordinated openings for the corresponding wood blocks to fit into. And, when it has a belly full, you push the dump lever to empty the truck and then begin all over again. A great activity for little ones. Has rope for pulling.

Size: 9" wide
17½" deep
10" high

Price List for Toy Plans

Page	Name	Price	Page	Name	Price
6-7-8	**The Depot** — Entire train complex. Patterns for people are included on all train plans.	$32.00	45	**Victoria Plan** Optional accessories packages. #1-(6) wood ornaments. #2-(2) pre-bent wood runners.	$10.00 7.50 40.00
	Rocky Mountain Express — Old time train.	7.00	46	**Spare Time**	2.50
	Mohawk Valley Railway — Work train with engine and 7 cars.	9.50	47	**3-in-1 Camper Truck**	9.00
	Federal Flyer — passenger train.	7.00	48	**Tenbeards**	3.50
	Victorian Station	4.00	49	**Bunker Hill**	5.50
	Freight Terminal	3.50	50	**The Family Circle**	4.00
	Depot Buildings and Accessories — Switching and water towers, waiting platform, crossings.	4.50	51	**The Commander Plan** Optional accessories package of 2 gears, 4 springs, 2 swivel-eye blocks.	8.50 13.00
	Level Crossing	3.50	52-53	**Roadgrader** **Turnapull**	6.00 6.50
14	**Leigh's Comfort Rocker**	7.00	58	**Sparky**	5.50
15	**Kerry's Stroller Plan** Optional accessories package of 2 wood ornaments, 4 rubber treads for wheels.	7.50 7.00	59	**Roundabout**	2.50
			60	**Amanda Plan** Optional accessories package of 4 wood ornaments.	6.00 8.00
16-17	**Fire Engine Plan** Patterns for people included. Optional accessories package of brass pipe fittings and 5 ft. of fire hose.	8.50 15.00	63	**Abigail Plan** Optional accessories package of 19 wood ornaments.	8.00 15.00
18	**Saturday Morning Moving Van**	7.00	64-65	**Stake Wagon Plan** Optional accessories package of 4 rubber treads for wheels.	9.50 10.00
23	**Elizabeth Cradle Plan** Optional accessories package #1 — (5) wood ornaments. Accessories package #2 — (4) 2½ ft. pcs. moulding for sides only.	8.00 11.00 24.00	66	**Yankee Clipper**	4.50
			68-69	**Hard Rock Mining Co.** Optional accessories package of ore car track rod, 15 ft. brass conveyor chain, 1 offset washer, 4 gears.	12.00 35.00
24	**Yellow Road School Bus** Pattern for people included.	8.50	70	**Box and Blocks**	4.00
25	**Sarah's Stove Plan** Optional accessories package of 4 wood ornaments, wood handles only, and 4 wood balls.	8.50 13.00	72	**Swedish Sled**	7.00
			76-77	**Ride Train Complete** Pattern for people included.	19.50
26	**Cupcakes and Tin, Cookies and Sheet**	2.50	78-79	**Engine and Coal Tender** **Coach** **Caboose** **Boxcar** **Gondola** Each plan includes crossing accessories and pattern for people.	6.50 4.50 4.50 4.00 3.50
27	**Birthday Cake Puzzle** **Pie and Bread Puzzles**	3.00 3.00			
28	**Rebecca's Icebox Plan** Optional accessories package of 4 hinges, 2 latches, and 1 name plate, all brass.	6.00 35.50	92	**Bumpy Road Convoy**	3.50
			94	**The Belly Full Dumper**	7.00
32-33	**Play Center Plan** Optional accessories package of 1 wood ornament, 2 wood handles.	8.50 6.50			
38	**Heidi's Hutch Plan** Optional accessories package of 5 wood ornaments.	8.50 9.00			
39	**Trestle Table and Chairs Plan** Optional accessories package of 6 wood ornaments.	8.50 9.50			

Please include $3.25 for postage and handling. Canadian orders $5.25 U.S. We prefer to send UPS, whenever possible, so include your street address.

Send plan orders to:
Timeless Designs
545 E. Milwaukee St.
Whitewater, WI 53190
Tel.: 1-800-765-0176
FAX: 414-473-6112

Check or money order in U.S. funds, MasterCard or Visa with order.